Power Where the Action Is

BOOKS BY HARVEY SEIFERT
Published by The Westminster Press

Power Where the Action Is

Conquest by Suffering: The Process and Prospects
of Nonviolent Resistance

Ethical Resources for International Relations
(Christian Perspectives on Social Problems)

Power

Where

the Action Is

by
HARVEY SEIFERT

THE WESTMINSTER PRESS
Philadelphia

LIBRARY OF CONGRESS CATALOG CARD No. 68–19898

BOOK DESIGN BY
DOROTHY ALDEN SMITH

Published by The Westminster Press ®
Philadelphia, Pennsylvania

PRINTED IN THE UNITED STATES OF AMERICA

Preface

WE STAND at the intersection of a new theology, a more useful social science, and a changing interest among churchmen. This book tries to bring some order out of the traffic from these three directions, for the benefit of the average church member in the ranks. The following chapters should provide fresh theological and sociological resources for decision and action in major areas of emerging concern on the job, in the community, and in politics.

Religious thought has often been excessively abstract, preoccupied with the past, and otherworldly. Recent emphases in theology are becoming more concrete and future-oriented. They are thoroughly immersed in the existing life of man and celebrate the unrealized possibilities in our secular urban civilization. After breaking the musty molds of useless antiquarian speculation, we are discovering new shapes for contemporary witness. There is renewed interest in this kind of theology which relates the major relevant core of our historical heritage to what God is calling us to be and do today.

Social and psychological scientists have accumulated vast amounts of supporting information, and they are paying more attention to the applied aspects of their research. These findings are essential to ethical decision. They also outline the strategy by which the average man could exert a much more significant influence on the world-shaping decisions of our time. The same explosion

5

in invention that brings society frozen food and moon probes also offers each individual new powers to shape human destiny. Much of this has been neglected and left unused. This book attempts to show how life may be given more momentous significance if we act on what it is possible for us to know.

A new breed of minister and layman is emerging. They are no longer content with generalities in preaching, unbelievable superstitions in doctrine, or moral hypocrisies in church and in society. With them it is no longer necessary to argue that religion should be related to life. Their question is how this can be done in the face of baffling complexities and immense concentrations of opposing power. How can one make ethical decisions? What style of life allows the most creative influence? What leverage points does the average man actually have in social decision-making? To these questions the following pages speak.

More theologically alert and better sociologically prepared, growing numbers of church members are taking their agenda for action from mid-twentieth-century human needs. They are insisting that the church become thoroughly involved in issues that really count, or they will walk out of the church. They are demanding the same careful, systematic inquiry in morals and religion as they have learned to expect in science and business. Conclusions simply based on ancient prescription, intuition, or common sense are not good enough. When it is disastrous to remain technological giants and ethical pygmies, they are insisting that our unbelievably rich social and religious resources be fully utilized for an unimaginably better life for man.

This book is based on a lifelong interest in theology and ethics, careful review of recent findings in social science, and innumerable conferences and discussion groups with laymen. To all these I am deeply indebted. I am particularly humbled before those laymen who are taking their Christian ministry seriously. They have found that where there is no great objective, life becomes muddled and melancholy. They are shaking loose from inadequate customs and habits. They are discovering new formulas for tired lives. These revitalized patterns restore verve, excitement, and creativity to Christian existence. They are beginning to unleash power where the action is.

H. S.

School of Theology at Claremont
Claremont, California

Contents

1

Invitation to Invasion

ONE of Charles M. Schulz's "Peanuts" comic strips had Sally merrily skipping rope. Suddenly she burst into tears. Sympathetic Linus asked: "What's the matter, Sally? What happened? Why are you crying?" Her reply was: "I don't know. I was jumping rope. Everything was all right when, I don't know, suddenly it all seemed so futile!"

Both suburbia and slum are full of people who identify with Sally. Modern man often feels himself to be helpless man. The events of life roll inexorably onward. All we can do is hang on. Individual action seems useless in the face of the immensity of mass social units and the complexity of our metropolitan and technological civilization. Decisions are repeatedly made by others, and yet they control us. Power seems inaccessible to the man in the street.

At the same time, this generation may well be impressed by decisive choices that must now be made. The decisions of a decade will now shape the destinies of the centuries. The destructiveness of modern military technology presents the greatest threat to human survival that the world has known. On the other hand, more mature international arrangements plus the peaceful uses of atomic energy may provide unimaginable new power sources for prolonging life and enriching culture. Because of the pressure of totalitarianism and the strains

11

within democracy, more freedom may now be lost by more
persons than at any other time in history. Recent social
inventions suggest alternatively that we may also be standing on the edge of a new birth of freedom for more men
in more areas of life than we have ever experienced before. The revolution of rising resentments in two thirds of
the world's population in underdeveloped areas may now
lead to unprecedented revolutionary turmoil. Or the attempt to bring exploding populations up to our standard
of living may lead to such resources depletion as to leave
this world a bleak, mined-out globe rotating through space.
Or, if we manage this matter well, our generation may be
remembered as the first in history to initiate the process
of successfully bringing the full benefits of civilization to
the entire human race.

In the face of such alternatives of danger and hope,
many of us feel overwhelmed by the unmanageability of
life. Ogden Nash wrote about "a minor literary figure"
whose life was "bespectacled and unspectacular." The title
given the poem was "The Nonbiography of a Nobody."
Yet this is not an inevitable portrait. One might also write
an essay entitled "Everybody Is Somebody." A sketch of
modern man as helpless is essentially a false picture, in
spite of all the elements of truth that are painted into it.
The average man does not need to be ineffectual. We are
powerless only by default. The truth of the matter is that
we can have significant influence on major public affairs.

Sociologically speaking, the pyramids of power are more
open than we think. Recent studies of social change reveal channels of influence which, if used by enough
average citizens, can be more effective than television
shows or expensive manipulations by public relations
firms. The Lazarsfeld studies of voting behavior, for example, have shown the importance of the "opinion leader,"
a person on any status level whose views are respected by
his peers. Opinions on public issues are changed with
particular effectiveness when there is a supporting small-

group experience, such as could be provided by the great multitude of classes and circles meeting each week in churches across the country. We have abundant resources that remain unused.

Furthermore, the man in the street does not need the advanced expertise of the specialist who is elected or employed to implement policy in detail. There is a level of competence that is both attainable and sufficient for the kind of general policy decisions in which it is appropriate for citizens to participate. The future is not fixed beyond hope of change. Democracy is not an idiot's dream, nor a museum curator's prize exhibit. It is, rather, a viable, powerful system for decision-making in which little men and big men can both participate.

Such personal influence, however, depends upon the adoption of a new style of life, much different from prevailing patterns. As a picture of current folkways, "Success Pattern—Twentieth-Century American" might be painted to show a man of distinction at ease in an overstuffed chair reading the sports page while a large-screen color television provided thrills for his children. The goal of life for many a man on the street, if filmed in a movie, might show the same congenial conformist rising as late as possible, leaving a wife as attractive as possible, driving to the office in a car as long as possible, working as briefly and pleasantly as possible, and returning to dinner and an evening's entertainment as fashionable and epicurean as possible. Then this reel would be indefinitely repeated —alarm clock, the office, dinner, movies, bed, alarm clock . . . Even three-dimensional photography could not conceal the shallowness of the pattern. With respect to the self-centered and limited values that this pattern stresses, life easily becomes surfeited and meaningless. It leaves an emptiness at the center of personality. As a pattern of existence it is at once too dull and too irresponsible. For a typical pattern we need to discover a style that is both more exciting and more adequate.

Our present customary patterns of life are not crudely destructive in the sense of directly burning homes, murdering children, or leaving a Hitlerian shambles to mark our steps. More indirectly and less openly we do nevertheless contribute to destruction and exploitation by our indifference. In the suburbs we are insulated from suffering. Poverty is for us a largely invisible social reality, hidden behind freeway landscaping or in isolated rural areas. We cannot bear to think about young men slogging through war-infested jungles and about snipers' bullets that shatter also the dreams of their wives back home. We look for escape in television and beer. We come to suffer from mass anesthesia. Our concerns become limited to family, lawn, and lodge. In a day when world-shaping decisions are being made, we echo Abbé Seyés, who, when asked what he did during the French Revolution, replied, "I survived." When we uncritically accept such a life-style, a high-fidelity, full-volume rendition of Martin Buber's words is in order: "If there were a devil, it would not be one who decided against God, but one who, in eternity, came to no decision."

Indifference actually contributes to the evil which it refuses to oppose. Inaction is a way of perpetrating injustice and exploitation. When Jesus asked, "Is it lawful on the sabbath to do good or to do harm?" (Mark 3:4), he cited all the options. It is one or the other. If we do not do good, we do evil. When we could pull a drowning person out of the water, as in the famous illustration of Camus, not to save life is to contribute to death. By nonparticipation in the social struggle we contribute to victory by the side we intellectually disagree with. Withholding active support from the side we do agree with leaves the opposition comparatively stronger. By doing nothing we alter the vectors of social force. When we do not vote we make it more likely that the candidate will win whom we would have opposed. The inactive citizen makes possible manipulation by oligarchs. He for whom life consists of work, wife, and whiskey becomes a proxy to be pocketed by those in power.

This is easily seen at crucial points in the past. We now quickly condemn anyone who sat on his hands during the period when Hitler was about to take over power. It is not so easy for us to see the crucial points at which we do the same thing. As long as more people crowd into football games than join peace organizations, so long can we expect the threat of war to continue. As Thoreau put it, "So we defend ourselves and our hen-roosts, and maintain slavery." Obadiah (v. 11) likewise said, "On the day that you stood aloof, . . . you were like one of them" (i.e., the looters of Jerusalem). This is an especially common vice of both the intellectual and the libertine. With respect to his flight from social responsibility, many a well-groomed, socially respected habitué of the best homes and country clubs has fallen into a particularly virulent type of immorality. Instead of making some contribution to pay his way in society, he is a parasite on the minority of humanity who are effective participants in social decision. We have been appalled by incidents in which bystanders did nothing while someone was openly being stabbed to death. This we say is despicable evidence of moral depravity. Yet we are not moved by the fact that we are standing idly by while not one person but rather millions of persons are being done to death by war, slow starvation, or imperialist and racist exploitation.

Not to speak when one should, or to speak irrelevantly; not to act when the battle is joined, or to act ineffectually —these are forms of sabotage as well as of sin. Subversive inactivity can become as dangerous as subversive activity. No man's life is exempt. When even inactivity is scored, every man counts for something, for or against. Ever since we moved so close to each other, modern life comes to each man as a demand for a verdict.

The positive point of this analysis is that the sensitive spirit does more than reject the temptation to behave destructively or to exist indifferently. He embraces a third level of life, the opportunity to live creatively. This concept of creativity adds a considerable plus element to the conventional pattern of living. We dare no longer be content to be typical teachers, machinists, or stenographers. The worker in factory or office has not done his full duty if he simply abstains from indecent language, slot machines, and strong drink. A home is not adequately filling its place in the community if it merely shelters beds for the parents and play space for the children. Conscripts of the Kingdom of God are called to be more than solid conventional citizens achieving a nominal income and no scandalous offspring, possessing a Rotary membership and no police record, or even teaching a church school class but with no further concern for social transformation. Creative living involves a more thoroughgoing reorientation of life.

This should be particularly clear to Christians who understand the message of their faith. The basic purpose for which we were created is to grow in the relationship of love toward God and neighbor. This is the all-absorbing preoccupation which Jesus insisted should involve all of one's heart and mind and strength. It is the single-mindedness which Kierkegaard described as the essence of purity of heart. This is authentic maturity. This would be man genuinely come of age.

The central aim of man's existence is not to accumulate much wealth or great prestige. Neither should our chief preoccupation be longevity or comfort. Instead, we follow one who "came not to be served but to serve" (Matt. 20:28). In Bonhoeffer's terms, each of us is likewise to be a "man existing for others." To live selfishly is to "lose" life (Matt. 16:25). It is only by a genuine, outgoing concern that, as an *unsought* by-product, we find spiritual growth and personal maturity, experience a rich depth of intimate fellowship with God and man, and contribute to ultimate values that have eternal significance.

Only by losing ourselves in the purposes of God, which include the fullest welfare of all men, do we find ourselves.

It is the Christian conviction that life is not lost by dying, but by living without awareness and commitment. The great secret about authentic life is that it must be open and outgoing, eager to learn what the situation is and energetic in response to need. A person who never discovers this secret ends his life without beginning it. He has lived a nonlife. When we do understand what things are all about, we know better where to focus our energies. The central reason for being is to give ourselves completely to such a part of God's eternal process of creation as is allowed to us.

Such an emphasis on creativity has particular meaning in our affluent times. For society and for individuals, full human potentialities emerge, not by egoistically enjoying past achievements, but by constructively facing the difficulties of making new social contributions. It is now an elementary lesson in history and sociology that civilizations remain strong and viable only as they meet crises with appropriate investments of creative energy. Either a problem-free situation or a lack of adequate response easily becomes the prelude to apathy and decline. The continuous renewal of dynamic culture requires persons willing to face the troubles of their times with some cost to themselves.

Now with the development of affluence, men are seriously tempted simply to enjoy the achievements of our forefathers without investing the creative energy necessary to multiply these gifts for our descendants. Many are now expressing the primacy of personal pleasure over social creativity through sexual indulgence, or the enjoyment of excessive luxury, or by becoming dropouts from functioning society. There is great danger that Las Vegas will replace Valley Forge as a symbolic expression of our national greatness.

Through past centuries the great challenge to work was

the production and distribution of material goods. This problem has not yet, of course, been completely solved on either a world or a national scale. But as we approach affluence, the provision of material things will not be nearly so demanding. If we are then to avoid decline for our civilization, we must increasingly respond to new ranges of problems to which we transfer much of the time and toil previously given to material matters. These new orders of problems are waiting to be seriously recognized, in the areas of social relationships and spiritual growth. The hours of leisure made possible by the automation of physical plenty now need to be channeled into world peace movements or aesthetic expression or prayer retreats. If this is done, strikingly new potentialities may be released within the generality of men. If this is not done, men will become dwarfed and culture dissipated. That is how things are. The world and man are made that way.

Not only does a right understanding of the meaning and purpose of existence drive us to these conclusions. Such a description of authentic life is also reinforced by a proper understanding of the meaning of religion. Recent theological emphases make it clear that religion is no longer to be thought of as a segment of life, but as a quality of our total existence. Once a separation was commonly made between the "religious" and the "secular." Into the secular portion of life were thrown man's activities in the marketplace and in city hall. The religious segment covered such activities as public worship or private prayer or tithing to the church budget. This understanding of religion could be portrayed graphically by two semi-circles drawn apart and with a zone of separation between. Such a schizophrenic portrayal is now seen as devilishly false. Religion has to do with the full orb of total existence. The difference it makes would have to be portrayed as two well-rounded circles, one above the other. To live religiously is to raise the level of every aspect of our being, placing each attitude and act under God. Religion is a way of living under the aspect of eternity, with constant regard for ultimate meanings.

Religion is more than spare-time activity. It is full-time activity. It makes a difference in every moment, at every place, and on every subject. The secular and the sacred are merged in a living unity. Karl Barth properly saw the Christian as continuously carrying the Bible in one hand and the daily newspaper in the other. Any man becomes a religious person only when the two are joined in his own being. Bonhoeffer correctly located the habitat of the church not at the edge but at the center of the city. Altars in a very real sense are to be built in the middle of Main Street.

One implication of this would be widely accepted among churchmen. Social scientists or politicians or citizens are not being religious when they simply describe or analyze the problems of man without involving interpretations of broader meaning and more ultimate issues raised by theology. When a person makes business decisions or studies political theory he is not practicing his religion unless he does it meditatively, in the light of the whole meaning of things, or the purposes of God.

Another equally important implication of a more adequate definition of religion is commonly avoided. We should be hit just as hard by the realization that we are not being religious when we discuss abstract possibilities about the character of God, memorize the books of the Bible, or consider the nature of moral goals, unless these are related to the concrete life of man. Contemplation of theological issues may become a substitute for Christian action in the world. Bible study unrelated to modern life may actually hide the message of the Bible. We are not even being religious when we pray, unless we intend that it make a genuine difference in our living.

There is no dedication to God without action among men. A tree is known by its fruits (Matt. 12:33). Confessing "Lord, Lord" is not enough. It must be accom-

panied by deeds (Matt. 7:21; Luke 6:46). One reason
for condemning the Pharisees is that "they preach, but
do not practice" (Matt. 23:3). Titus 1:16 provides a
summary judgment: "They profess to know God, but they
deny him by their deeds; they are detestable, disobedient,
unfit for any good deed."

Furthermore, there is no authentic worship of God
without service to neighbor. Amos 5:21-24 might be
paraphrased as saying that God hates and despises our
worship services and that he is not listening to our organ
preludes and hymns and prayers, because we are not
practicing justice and righteousness. Jesus likewise emphasized that if we are offering our gifts at the altar and
remember that we have not dealt rightly with a brother,
we had better rush out of the sanctuary and first be recon-
ciled to our brother before coming back to complete our
worship (Matt. 5:23-24). Ostentatious public prayers
are a mockery when hypocritically spoken (Matt. 6:5).
A person can actually be more religious than that in smoke-
filled caucus rooms of political conventions provided he is
prayerfully trying to express what he believes to be the
word of God to that situation.

Churches with large-view windows behind the altar
always look out on the beauty of trees, sky, or mountains.
They never face slums or amusement parks or factories.
It would be just as appropriate to do the latter as the
former. The revelation of God can be seen in the beauties
of nature. It can also be seen in the courageous life of man
in ugly or forbidding surroundings. We are always
tempted to label as religious something that pulls our attention away from dirty people or prosaic daily occurrences. Thereby we may delay our meeting with God.
Many a suburbanite during his meditation in church
treats social problems only as distant thunder on a Sunday
afternoon—not enough to interrupt his picnic. By this
kind of worship he is avoiding God. We may refuse to
admit it openly, but in actual practice religion as we in-

terpret it often has little to do with human affairs. At such times we can be sure that God has little to do with our religion.

God is continuously interested in his world. He created it, has purposes for it, and remains active within it. If God is to be found, we will experience him in the world. If we are to establish relationships with him, we must join him in the world. The reconciling action of God occurs in the world of industrial work and political decision. Interest in the secular world is not a retreat from faith, but rather an appropriation of a fuller faith which accepts its responsibility for the world's future.

For any generation there is no service of God except in the existing world. Decision is always contemporary. Here and now, the commitment of the churchman is to be expressed in every place he stands, including leisure hours as well as working hours, intimate relationships and the massive impersonal structures of society. This definitely pushes him beyond like-minded companionship within the church into those regions where winds blow hard and "outsiders" dominate. Christians quite properly gather in the church for preparation and renewal. Neither of these can fully occur, however, unless Christians also scatter out of the church to every point of serious human need. The authentic Christian always lives an exposed life, out where the traffic is moving or the bombs dropping. He does not thereby move away from God. Instead, God also stands in the world and calls us to come to him there. God is to be encountered wherever men live and struggle. God is the Lord of the church, but also of the hospital, the city hall, the assembly line, and the executive suite.

For the sake of excitement or to gain relief from monotony, it is no longer necessary to read about revolutions in a newspaper or to run to a fire. One can find significance and meaning close at hand. At every major point at which he touches the world, each honest Christian has enlisted for invasion. In joining the church he has volunteered for a peaceful penetration which inch by inch, decision by decision, contributes to the conversion of culture. Life becomes intriguing and important because it is tied to an enterprise no less consequential than that.

This can be true for every man, not only for a few fortunate or chosen ones. Within the church the most significant contributions are no longer the monopoly of the clergy. This is a clear implication of the current theology of the laity which sees no higher place in the church than that occupied by the average layman. If religion is now to be seen as interpenetrating the common life, then the layman who works in the world is the most significant representative of the church. Ministers exist to help laymen do the work of the church in the world, instead of laymen existing to help the minister do the work of the church inside the sanctuary. The Reformation doctrine of the priesthood of all believers is now expressed in a new renaissance of the laity. Every layman has a divine calling. There is no superior status. If the church is to witness and to serve, it is the laity who are to witness and to serve. For the lonely prophet of Biblical times, we are finding it necessary in mass society to substitute the prophetic group. Instead of the priest set apart for counsel, we are learning the rewards of the therapeutic fellowship.

Much of the work of the church can be done only by laymen. They alone bring the advanced specialized competences which are essential in the modern world. Paul's list of differing gifts (Eph. 4:11-12; I Cor. 12:4-13) can now be given new meaning as we consider the varieties of resources brought by physicists, psychologists, and philosophers. Furthermore, laymen alone fully know the dilemmas presented by the world. Out of their involvement in life in its many ramifications they can more competently list the questions to be answered. It is laymen in particular who feel the tension between the church and an uncongenial or hostile world. They have to take the brunt of the encounter between unrealized norms and existing realities. Laymen alone are present in most of the relationships of men. At many points of crucial decision, the church can be represented only through the laity. So far as the Christian community is concerned, no one else is there. Laymen carry on most of the dialogue between the church and the world. They will be listened to in those quarters in which the accepted stereotype of the clergy-man is so negative that his words are useless. When they are at their jobs, laymen are giving full-time Christian ser-vice. Through their daily contacts they are the channels for God's redemptive power.

The worldly mission of the laity is illuminated by new insights drawn from the traditional Christian concept of the calling. This doctrine of vocation looked upon one's daily activity as a life task set by God. The call to salva-tion was related to the divine calling to a worthwhile oc-cupation. The Protestant Reformers saw this as equally true for both so-called secular and sacred occupations. They gave religious approval to constructive worldy ac-tivity. Professional employees of the church were no longer to be considered somehow closer to God's favor. On the contrary, fishermen, housewives, businessmen, and pro-fessors could stand as near to the altar of God as could ministers or monks.

Now this doctrine is to be expanded to leisure as well as to work, and to political as well as economic activity. In all these ways our life energies can be related to im-portant social purposes. All constructive work then be-comes a living, daily offering to God. It introduces a holy meaning even into humdrum routine. It was a monastic insight that to labor is to pray. Work may be a way of worshiping God, a spontaneous expression of love and gratitude.

Such a union between worship and work comes when we recognize God's call in man's need. The equation for translating this into personal decisions might be written: a social need plus a personal capacity equals a divine call.

Whatever is required by man is what God would have
done. Whatever I am able to do is what I should do. The
doors of opportunity in this respect often open downward
to the areas in which the greatest social need is found.
Benjamin Franklin once said, "Where liberty dwells,
there is my country." Thomas Paine replied, "Where liberty is not, there is mine!" The agenda for individual
action is found in the pattern of need in the contemporary
world.

Our response is to be continuous, systematic, method-
ical, and vigorous. In terms of the traditional doctrine of
vocation, it involves what Max Weber describes as *inner-
weltliche,* or "within the world," asceticism. The doctrine
of vocation intensifies our motivation and calls for a serious, energetic response. Historically the idea came to carry
with it a tremendous drive. A critic of the church once
said, "I had rather meet a regiment with drawn swords
coming out against me than one Calvinist who believes he
is doing the will of Almighty God!" In recent years, however, this doctrine seems to have lost much of its vitality.
Max Weber wrote, "The idea of duty in one's calling
prowls about in our lives like the ghost of dead religious
beliefs." Current conditions cry for a resurrection of the
idea of vocation in ways appropriate to our techno-urban
situation.

Our enlarged leisure demands new discoveries in the
avocational meaning of the doctrine of the calling. Outside of working hours for which we are paid, each of us
has a great deal of discretionary time, the use of which
we ourselves determine. This may be crowded full, but
we have chosen the items with which it is stuffed. Eve-
nings, longer weekends, and more extended vacations can
be spent either on the trivial or on the tremendous. Even
though presented with new gifts of such personalized
time, our generation still has a low leisure competence.
With more time on our hands, we fill it with mediocrities
to avoid admitting that we do not know what to do with

it. Greater leisure shows up an empty life as searchlights in the night pitilessly illuminate a prison yard.

The sum total of the spare time available to the members of any congregation would provide them with a good many additional lifetimes. One hundred years of work can be crowded into fifty years of life by doubling the efficiency or the perspicacity with which we use our time. A seriously creative orientation should produce less attention to socially useless hobbies and more to community-building activity. While some recreation is necessary for creative living, investment of leisure time needs to go beyond gin rummy or matchbook-collecting to focus also on the scourges of war, poverty, or discrimination. Unless from time to time one does something like carry a petition from door to door, one should not be considered a normal human being in modern society. For the churchman it will become as important to talk to one's mayor or congressman as to teach a church school class, or to address envelopes for a United Nations Association mailing as to put a church envelope in the offering plate.

With the gift of the new leisure and of labor saving by cybernetics, not only homemakers but many of the rest of us can have a double career. Wives are already adding schoolroom or social-work agency to kitchen. Their husbands are discovering the possibilities in "moonlighting" for extra income. In these more affluent days both men and women can increasingly make their second full-time career one of volunteer service in the community, adding youth-serving agency or political party to factory or office or kitchen. The calling of a social-change agent may now more realistically become one of the professions of us all.

Christians must act like this or acknowledge their unbelief and apostasy. This is an essential part of what religion is really about. For the Christian, there is no escaping an invasion into the world—not hesitatingly or cynically or partially, but joyfully and lustily and fully. Churchmen must get into politics and reform movements and economic pressure groups, wherever God in a particular decade is working, because they also know that is what the world is largely about.

Often Christians are already there. The churchman has a thousand faces. He is already engaged as a businessman in his office, a worker on the assembly line, or a homemaker in the kitchen. He may now be a member of one of a long list of community-building organizations—churches, parent-teacher associations, fraternal orders, or reform groups. He is already a citizen participating in public discussion, supporting a political party, and periodically checking his ballot in a polling booth. Because he does these things he stands at the threshold of social power.

Yet characteristically he does not step across the threshold because he lacks skill. He does not know what to do or how to do it. Or he hesitates to join religious faith to daily activity. Church members now live in every block, work in every plant, participate in every political decision, yet it is hard to see them. They are not acting like Christians. Contemporary churchmen have low visibility because, chameleon-like, they have taken on the protective coloration of their environment. With a religion derived from culture rather than from Christ, they are conspicuously inconspicuous. If they are to be true to the demands of modernity and of their religious calling, churchmen must now adopt a pattern of life more adequate and creative than is customary. Such a life-style will involve radical renovation for some. As sensitivity increases it will require considerable change for all.

That is what this book is all about. What is the method for relating the Christian faith to concrete human problems? What is the uniquely Christian approach to on-the-job decisions, or to participation in community-building organizations, or to political action? To these matters the following chapters will attempt to speak.

2
Making Ethical Decisions

"CAN the Christian Be in Business?" is the title of the first chapter in Harold L. Johnson's *The Christian as a Businessman* (Association Press, 1964). The same question might be asked about politics or community participation in general. All of these are realms of conflict and compromise. There is an initial apparent contradiction between the action of love appropriate to the Christian and the kinds of conduct often necessary to stay in business. Yet, as the best thinkers in ethics would do, this professor of economics answers his question in the affirmative. Christians are called to participate in highly ambiguous enterprises that are necessary to human welfare.

In doing so, we need to be highly realistic about the relationship between Christian goals and practical possibilities. Otherwise, we may use the gospel as a hallucinatory drug and spend our energies in pursuing a mirage. As a matter of fact, naïve utopianism often leads to results quite opposite to those intended. In trying to do what cannot be done, we are likely to make no contribution to what can be done.

We are always limited to the best that can be done within the given situation. Available choices are restricted by existing resources, the claims of many different values, and the actions of others. To escape a nagging wife or a falling bomb we cannot choose to jump to the moon. The businessman must often limit his humanitarian generosity for the sake of avoiding bankruptcy. A citizen cannot have his way in national policy so long as most other citizens disagree with him. Even Jesus could not both heal on the Sabbath and retain the goodwill of the Pharisees. There are no slick solutions. In an imperfect world we ordinarily have to choose not between blacks and whites but between shades of gray.

Utopian sermons do not help much. Laymen listening to demands for immediate perfection know they cannot live that way on Monday—and that the minister, if he is really sensitive to all the values and complexities of life, cannot even live that way on Sunday. Since our calling is found within the secular world, our duty is to do the best possible within the imperfect circumstances of that world. We must choose, from among the options which actually exist, that course of action which moves farthest in the direction of ideal goals. This is doing the present will of God in the place in which we are set to serve. God does not require the impossible. He does require the most constructive.

It is also true that we need to keep the tension tight between the norm and our realistic choice. Action is held back by the force of circumstances. At the same time, the forward pull of the goal must be strongly asserted. Otherwise one is tempted to assume that nothing much better is possible than what is already being done. This kind of capitulation actually identifies the requirements of the Christian faith with the prevailing practices of contemporary culture. Such "culture religion" is death to vital faith. The Christian word to the world is always "yes," since we immerse ourselves in its possibilities. The word is also "no," because we cannot approve the world totally as it exists. As George Webber says, we must "go native in all things save faith and morals."

While we are obliged to do that which is possible, we are also obligated to do the very best that is possible—and that is always something more than average practice. Before the righteousness of God, even the finest act of the noblest man falls short. We need always to be searching for a better way than we have yet discovered. A distinguishing mark of the Christian is the direction of his movement. Conscientious laymen are always leaning in the direction of those alternatives which improve conditions. They should always be the first to adopt a new policy that promises to be a fuller expression of the norm of love. They never exert influence merely by affable adapting, but always by insistently instigating. There is an adventurous quality about Christian ethical decision, which takes some risks in novel experimentation. The responsible choice is one that contributes creativity amid ambiguity, and invention wherever there is imperfection.

The Christian therefore expects often to find himself in a creative minority, pushing beyond the average or the typical. Because he is a partisan of progress the unusually creative person is likely to experience varying degrees of misunderstanding, resistance, or opposition. Any man who moves on the frontier is likely to be attacked. Hesitancy about such consequences easily causes weak men to back down from forward-looking decisions. If moral choice is not to be perverted by fear, it must be marked by boldness. The Christian stance contrasts markedly with the prevailing preference for merging with the mass without sweat or idiosyncrasy. We often need to recall the judgment of Jesus, "Woe to you, when all men speak well of you" (Luke 6:26).

If we take these matters with full seriousness, it becomes important to improve our skill in decision-making. Every day brings a new series of choices—whether or not to work, to buy caviar, to write a congressman. The shape of the future is being determined by the quality of choices in the present. It is no good to think that all our problems will be automatically solved by affluence, the pill, or one or two easy political panaceas. We require a more muscular moral methodology to refine the aims and actions of our society. How are we to make competent ethical choices within the sharp dilemmas posed by modern techno-urban culture? In arriving at such conclusions, the thoughtful Christian customarily takes into account three elements.

The first of these is the Christian theological perspective. This is not always taken seriously enough. In a church-sponsored group of bankers, one participant suggested a fuller exploration of the theological implications of the matter under discussion. Another commented, "Things are bad enough already without getting them mixed up with theology!" In our more sober moments, we know that we must get all moral questions thoroughly mixed up with theology.

Churchmen ought never face ethical dilemmas simply as bewildered citizens of a particular country, or as prisoners of the limited perspective of a single class or race, but as Christians who have basic insights about the nature of the whole. For us the total response of faith is shaped by beliefs about God, the nature of man, and the meaning of salvation. God is the creator of mankind and the lord of history. He is the righteous and powerful sovereign over men and nations. We find ourselves under his judgment, and he provides for us also a ground for hope. God is the universal father—not a tribal deity. All men stand alike before his judgment and mercy. He loves each of us with full overflowing love which goes far beyond anything we deserve.

Man is a center of worth with tremendous potentialities for good and for evil. He is a sinner who can become a saint. He finds his true destiny, the purpose for his living, in responsible use of his freedom under God. This being the case, any social program must both restrict expressions of human evil and stimulate the development of man's propensities toward good. Democracy, for example, requires laws to be enforced against antisocial acts, at the same time that it encourages free expression and majority decision in the making of those laws. In Reinhold Niebuhr's famous aphorism, "Man's capacity for justice makes democracy possible; but man's inclination to injustice makes democracy necessary."

Included also among the theological realities that we affirm is the overarching norm of love. As God loves us, so we are to love our neighbors, near and far. The primary motivation of action should be, not self-interest or limited goodwill, but wholehearted altruism sensitive to the needs of all men and willing to go to the lengths of self-sacrifice where that is necessary. Love in its full Christian meaning is all-inclusive in its scope and even gives priority to the needs of the neighbor.

Such theological realities make a profound difference in moral choice. For one thing, they contribute a stronger motivation for social action. Any obstacle placed in the path of man becomes a monstrous evil when viewed from the perspective of God. He who is deeply committed sees service of neighbor as related to the purpose of life, the destiny of man, and authentic human existence. It is as centrally significant as all that. When anyone begins deeply and genuinely to love others even as God has loved us, he is urgently impelled to corresponding action.

Theological beliefs can also bring the gift of a source of power beyond the material and the present. When campaigns get rough and action meets opposition, decisions are likely to be less distorted by caution and rationalization if we are not depending on our own resources alone. Through the centuries, religious experience has brought sustaining strength to many a supporter of righteous lost causes. In spite of the skepticism of secularistic man, an awareness of a transcendent dimension of life can still do the same for us. The adulation of men is not so necessary and defeat is not so discouraging to the person who experiences a supporting "I-Thou" relationship with God. Necessary attributes of courage and persistence are more firmly rooted when they grow out of convictions about the basic nature of reality.

Theological grounding, taking into account the whole of things, provides a greater comprehensiveness of information that ought to lead to more valid conclusions. It makes a great deal of difference whether God is benevolent or malevolent, whether man can or cannot do good, and what, if anything, is the meaning of life. This is basic data for adequate decision. This view of more ultimate reality should deliver us from private biases and perverted perspectives. Any less complete data can be expected to lead to false or inadequate decisions. Each of us is the captive of a particular place or time. Release from the prejudices of a limited perspective is the beginning of social wisdom.

We need strong, deep theological roots in order to clarify our goals. Thin theology makes fragile ethics. Only as we see what is ultimately most important can we know what is immediately most urgent. Unless we are clear about the meaning of life, even our most thrilling discoveries can become what Thoreau called a new railroad in his community, "an improved means toward an unimproved end." At the moment, the conquest of the atom seems more likely to bring us to atomic destruction than to atomic prosperity, and the same air transport that could bind the world together is employed in blasting it apart. Man's proudest powers have also become his greatest sources of peril, or as Sir Winston Churchill more colorfully put it, "The Stone Age may return on the gleaming wings of science." The shallow and slippery soil of a superficial scientism does not easily produce the finest flower of moral responsibility. The urge to expediency is too great, with its passion for quick returns in the form of short-run tangible objectives. Such a preoccupation with instrumental values and relative goals has allowed us to enshrine national aims as eternal values and group interests as the absolute good. In the words of General Omar N. Bradley: "The world has achieved brilliance without wisdom, power without conscience. Ours is a world of nuclear giants and ethical infants."

A second element entering into responsible moral decision is ethical principles. These are sometimes called laws or guidelines, or middle axioms, with somewhat varying shades of meaning with regard to specificity or finality. Yet these terms fit within the same category of statements about the meaning of morality that are more specific than the norm of love and yet more general than concrete decisions. Principles are general guides to action which grow out of religious insight or out of experience in actualizing values. They include such implications of love as truthtelling, loyalty to one's pledged word, the supremacy of human personality over economic goods, liberty, equality of opportunity, brotherhood, or peace. The use of such principles is being minimized these days by the so-called contextualists in ethics. Their fears are, however, unfounded if we recognize that we do not find in ethical principles a system of minute rules to cover every conceivable action. We see here only guideposts pointing direction, the more specific meaning of which must be found in the immediate situation. Furthermore, we are dealing here with a system of principles and values which must be applied as a whole, each to be modified by the other rather than in too simple a fashion, taking only one into account at any given time. For example, when a decision is made to introduce automation, there are numbers of values that must be considered. One might accelerate automation for the sake of providing material goods for consumers, or one might delay it for the sake of providing employment for workers in the industry. Some weight must be given to both considerations.

With this kind of understanding of their meaning, principles are necessary if we are to know what is the good which we are to seek for others. Especially in novel or complex situations we need such guidance lest we leave love without meaningful content, and rationalize its meaning according to private preference or the pressures of current custom. Love may be interpreted in quite opposite ways. It has been thought consistent with aristocratic, hierarchical structures of inequality, with some expression of charity by those at the top. With this view one can more easily defend segregation as a pattern for race relations. On the other hand, if as a principle or general summary of experience, we see weaknesses in paternalism, and if we consider brotherhood or equal opportunity more valid versions of the norm, we would tend to insist upon unsegregated patterns.

Each situation is not so completely unique as radical contextualists would claim it to be. There are enough likenesses within classes of situations that we can helpfully generalize about them. A man does not have to start all over again each time he sees a parked car he would like to have or each time he is alone with an attractive woman. If in such contexts we recall principles about stealing or adultery, our decisions have better grounding and are less subject to the irrational impulse of the moment. That such guiding principles are necessary is further demonstrated by the fact that even contextualists do begin to use them in actual practice when they analyze concrete choices.

One helpful way of summarizing a group of guidelines is in a modification of a chart that Paul Ramsey used in his *Basic Christian Ethics* (Charles Scribner's Sons, 1950). Adding an additional dimension to his original two-dimensional representation, we can say that there are three questions to which we need generalized answers, covering the what, when, and where of moral choice. To describe what the good is that ought to be sought, a scale of values is helpful. This can be represented by an arrow pointing upward. At the bottom would be placed lower physical and material values. In the intermediate position might be put the various values in social relationships, while at the top would come intellectual, moral, aesthetic, and religious values. From the Christian perspective all these values are to be sought. Physical health, family loyalty, and relationship with God are all good. Whenever in a given situation there is a contradiction between the claims of different values, however, the highest are to be stressed as the most important. As Jesus pointed out, there are times when families have to be left for the sake of serving God. The total range of values can contribute to the fulfillment of persons, but a coherent system of values requires that the highest be given priority.

A horizontal arrow, intersecting the first and pointing to the right, might be drawn to represent the time span through which values are to be sought, with short-run consequences placed at the left end and long-run consequences at the head of the arrow to the right. There are often significant differences between the two. Quantities of alcohol, for example, may bring a few hours of euphoria, with a hangover the next morning and marital difficulties the next year. Logging too many hills may increase immediate lumbering profits, but leave no wood for future generations. Again, the full listing of all short-term and long-term consequences is to be considered, but when a choice must be made, long-continuing outcomes are to be more heavily weighted.

A third arrow might be used, pointing away from the reader in a third dimension—that of depth. This would represent the question of for whom values are to be sought. If at the nearer end a man places himself and at the farther end his neighbors, again whenever values are abundant enough to go around, they may be actualized for both self and others. But especially in dealing with scarce values the thrust of Christian love is toward priority for neighbors.

To summarize this particular set of general principles, we should aim to realize the fullest possible range of values for the most possible persons over the longest possible period of time, but with emphasis on higher values, long-run consequences, and the fulfillment of others. In terms of our diagram an effect of the Christian faith is to lengthen each of the three arrows, including in higher values the relationship to God of the saint, including in

the range of love even enemies, and adding to longer consequences the dimension of eternity. We are to move insistently toward the top, right, and distant ranges of this
three-dimensional representation.

How are these criteria to be related to concrete decisions? This moves us to the third major element in ethical
decision, namely, sociological data. In addition to fundamental understandings about life and somewhat more specific guideposts, we need information about the unique
situation in which we act. This kind of understanding is
almost entirely derived from the social sciences (or more
properly, the behavioral sciences, including the psychological disciplines). Every man has some information he
has learned from his own personal experience or from his
informal contact with the experiences of others. The
thoughtful man will also try to secure more systematically
accumulated research findings on the level of competence
appropriate to his limited sphere of action as a layman and
citizen. Such data about contemporary life provides information about the nature of the situation, as well as a
more exact definition of the problem. It makes possible a
more comprehensive listing of the possible alternative
solutions and a more reliable understanding of the consequences of each—including those outcomes which are
due to the motivation of the actor and the inherent nature
of the act, as well as the impact on its social setting. All
these elements are essential to any decision that goes beyond wishful thinking or ignorant guessing. An accurate
understanding of the cultural situation is important to any
sound comprehension of what the problem really is. Fo-
cusing on the essential elements inherent in the problem
is a prerequisite to any serious discussion of possible solutions. A full listing of options is necessary if we are to
avoid settling for a second-best. When we understand the
probable outcomes of various alternative choices, we can
compare each set of consequences with the values or goals
set by our theological and ethical insights. Responsible de-

cision then means adoption of the alternative, the antici-
pated consequences of which most closely approximate the
aims of the Christian faith. These ends of person-fulfill-
ing love we believe also to be the purposes of God.

One cannot make responsible decisions without this
kind of use of specific, empirical information. Social data
is indispensable to Christian conduct. Those who dispar-
age or deemphasize the contribution of the social sciences
are removing churchmen from contemporary witness. They
are taking an escape route from mission to the world. This
can be more easily seen in the case of complex or controversial matters. Without the help of social science how
can one know the general policy necessary to avoid depressions, or the most efficient way to relieve poverty, or which
of vigorously debated approaches to foreign policy is best?
A person is that much less a witness to his faith if he does
not accurately understand the precise nature of such problems. Without some homework he cannot even know the
full range of alternatives from among which he might
choose. Nor can he make a choice until he has the essential available information about what the probable consequences of each alternative would be. In each situation
there is an option which is the best possible under the
circumstances. Uncovering it calls for both theological
and sociological tools.

Instead of this careful creative approach, the religious
mind has frequently cherished unfounded legends, supported irrelevant proposals, and dissipated energy into ill-
chosen campaigns. When "love is blind" a person intend-
ing to do good may actually do harm. He then aggravates
what he is attempting to cure. The religious man may
then become a greater menace than the outright criminal,
for he supports a false position with enthusiastic devotion,
and he cloaks it with such idealism as more easily to de-
ceive his hearers. Those whose disposition is thoroughly
altruistic especially need to avoid the naïve, sentimental
urge to act without data. In addition to being fervent and

sincere, love must also be wise and informed. Just as certain activities should not be undertaken without benefit of clergy, so conclusions on social matters should not be reached without benefit of social scientists.

A decision-making process informed by theological, ethical, and sociological materials can be illustrated by a case study drawn from our area of responsibility as citizens. Probably the most urgent problem we face in this field is that of peaceful international relations.

The Christian approaches such a problem with the theological conviction that a loving Father is deeply concerned about each of his people who are ravaged by war and by international aggression or exploitation. If we are to serve God, we must commit energies to the elimination of war and the protection of justice. Our religious faith, while noting the propensity of man to conflict, also sees enough possibilities for good in man to conclude that conflict does not have to take the form of war. Into a community of love, war breaks as a disruptive obscenity. We are confident that a greater embodiment of love in structures of justice would create more tolerable international conditions. Our obligation is to discover what such structures might be. The central purpose for our being is realized only as we devote ourselves seriously to this kind of enterprise.

All this should add up to powerful motivation and basic guidance for action. When men devote their highest scientific capacities to perfecting methods for destroying mankind, this is morality standing on its head. It is a form of fighting against God. If we were willing to burst through the confining and distorting aspects of prevailing custom, and genuinely to immerse ourselves in such theological realities, the results would be as phenomenal now as they have been in other moments in history when men took their religion seriously. If each churchman read the daily paper in the frame of reference of God and his will, there would be less subsequent clicking on of television sets and much more dialing of telephones and attending of planning meetings. There would be such a rush to join the peace movement that politicians would have to recognize a brand-new social climate—or else be swept from office as too ancient for their times. The fact that this is not the case indicates that dedication to God is not the central force in our lives. Spontaneous, outgoing response to God's greatness and love and to the need of men is largely only a theory among us. Theological belief is superficially decorative instead of genuinely internalized and profoundly moving.

A great deal of wisdom is stored up in the Bible and elsewhere in the form of relevant ethical principles. These remind us, for example, that a proper aim for action is the realization, for all men, of economic and social order and opportunity, as a prerequisite to the growth of higher values. We are also informed that, all other things being equal, violence involves evils which tend to be self-defeating, and that competitive selfishness limits the full possibilities of community. Generalized principles would also remind us of the necessity of acting realistically, taking the longest steps possible under the circumstances. To take on effective meaning which makes any contemporary difference, such principles must be integrated with sociological findings. As pointed out in the preceding chapter, religion by definition joins ultimate concerns and daily dilemmas. The most fruitful discussion of decision-making interweaves ethical principles and sociological data.

Social scientists describe our politico-economic situation and define the issues. Briefly summarized, they point out that ours is a world of nation-states, each acting in its own national interest and each claiming national sovereignty. Among sovereign states, major conflicts of interest repeatedly lead to arbitrament by arms. Political scientists also outline the major alternatives from among which we might choose a remedy. We might attempt peace through

domination by a single nation, as in a *pax Americana,* or
we might rely on deterrence, or a balance of power, or
we might strengthen international organization, involving
collective security and provision for peaceful change.

Both behavioral science and ethical principles help us
evaluate the various alternatives. The consequences of
peace imposed by a dominating nation or a small group of
nations include denial of freedom and stimulation to revolution. Deterrence may be a temporarily effective stop-
gap, but for various reasons it is unstable and undepend-
ably effective as a long-term policy. It also raises serious
ethical questions about the relationship of means to ends
or the relationship of threat to understanding. The international organization approach has much to recommend it
sociologically as an extension of democratic procedures
and collective controls to the world level. In ethical terms
international organization may be thought of as a structure
for brotherhood on a world scale, an instrument for universal cooperation for the common good.

The economic aspects of international relations simi-
larly illustrate the fruitfulness of joining ethical and sociological factors. Love for neighbor must be expressed
also to the distant poor. We who have experienced the
unmerited grace of God should, of all persons, respond
with gratitude in service to need. Such service includes
material as well as spiritual aid, since physical things are
of indispensable instrumental value. Christian love asks
the fortunate to assign priority to their neighbors' needs.
The cross calls us to a kind of sacrifice scarcely ever apparent in our Cadillac culture. In the economy of God,
need anywhere constitutes a claim on resources everywhere. Altruism should find an international as well as
an interpersonal expression. "If any one has the world's
goods and sees his brother in need, yet closes his heart
against him, how does God's love abide in him?" (I John
3:17.)

This is explosive material when combined with contemporary sociological statistics. Social research describes the existing situation of inequality with two thirds of the world's population in undeveloped areas with tragically lower-than-average standards of living. Political scientists point to economic nationalism as a basic factor in poverty and war. They also describe major alternatives and their consequences. We could continue economic nationalism with whatever immediate profits it brings us, and eventually reap the consequences of the rising revolution of resentments in the new nations. Or we could support responsible programs of international economic development. If we are to do the latter, there are stubborn economic realities to be faced. Raising standards of living in undeveloped areas requires industrialization, which demands capital. If capital is not to be sweated out of native populations under totalitarian auspices, such capital must come from abroad. Because of the magnitude of the requirements and the nonprofit nature of many of the investments needed (as in schools, public-health measures, or river development), private investment must be supplemented by government aid from countries such as our own. Such assistance programs must be supplemented by appropriate trade policies and by encouragement of social and economic reform in developing nations. Technologically, it is possible to eliminate mass poverty everywhere in the world. What is yet necessary is a union of religious motivation and sociological knowledge in more energetic and imaginative action.

At the moment, both theological guidance and sociological guidance sometimes seem confused. Statements made by one school of thought cancel out those made by another. However, this is largely a surface turbulence, due to the fact that we are still growing in our understandings. Some disagreement inevitably accompanies new development. At the same time, there is now considerable consensus about method and fundamental viewpoint. In many respects our generation is better equipped for making its decisions than has been true in any previous time. We know better how to help one another through a group-sharing of insights. The recent ferment of theological discussion and the amazing development of methodology and findings in the social and psychological sciences have placed unparalleled resources at our disposal.

Decision-making becomes more manageable also because involvement in momentous universal matters can be broken down into day-to-day actions of individual persons, each in a particular location and vocation. The next chapter will consider how this method of ethical analysis may be used in the on-the-job decisions related to our daily vocations. Later chapters will deal with our participation as citizens in community organizations and politics. Work and citizenship are inescapable involvements of responsible living. So long as we want to stay alive and to live in groups, we must do some economic work and maintain the requisite social order. Resources from recent research should help us do a considerably better job in relating the fundamental materials of theology to these basic essentials for human society.

3
On-the-Job Dilemmas

THE CENSUS BUREAU maintains a list of some thirty thousand identifiable jobs, including "tea-bag stringer" (who ties tags to the bags), "thumb cutter" (who has something to do with globe manufacture), and "frit maker" (who would obviously seem to make frits). In one or another strange or common occupation each fully employed person spends more of his waking hours on the job than in any other single activity. Here he makes a major input of his life energies to produce an output of goods and services that either contribute to or detract from the common life. More than that, he affects the general climate of economic and social institutions by the choices he makes on the job. A man may not have a vote in the United States Senate, and he may not control the labor policies of the South African diamond mines, but he does have an effective vote on the quality and craftsmanship on a particular painting job, or on the environment for learning in a specific classroom, or on the parental influence on a particular child.

God is to be served only in the particular time and place in which a person stands. God cannot be obeyed by us as though we were citizens of Pakistan. The neighbor is not to be served as though we were millionaires. We cannot be satisfied to meet the problems of our situation as though we were nineteenth-century men. Our role is to be played at the spot on the stage on which we stand.

In his particular living place every man plays several roles. He may be family man or school boy, playboy or recreational man, churchman or businessman. For the latter category, "vocational man" would be a more satisfactory designation in order to include persons in all occupations including labor, management, professional people, and homemakers. Whatever his position, every conscientious Christian has the opportunity of relating a religiously informed decision-making process to his particular on-the-job dilemmas.

While we probably spend more time at work than on any other activity, we are also likely to have related the job less to religious insight. This may be because the church has not talked much about on-the-job problems. A significant survey of 1,700 businessmen was reported by Raymond C. Baumhart in the July–August, 1961, issue of *Harvard Business Review*. When asked how much guidance their church or clergymen had provided for their ethical problems, 35 percent answered "None." An additional 25 percent checked "Some, but not enough." For one reason or another, 23 percent preferred not to express an opinion. This left only 16 percent checking "About right amount," and only 1 percent who thought that too much guidance had been provided. C. A. Gerstacker, chairman of the board of Dow Chemical Company, in a recent address said: "One of the traditions of the church seems to be that business and business problems are only referred to, usually in a polite and casual way, but they are not actually talked about. . . . I suggest to you that it is time for . . . the church to help us apply the Christian faith to actual business problems. . . . I think the church has much to offer us in industry, and I also think the church needs to offer a little more of what we need and a little less of what we want."

The troubled conscience of businessmen, scientists, and other vocational persons is quite evident in our time. For example, Benjamin M. Selekman, professor at Harvard's

Graduate School of Business Administration, reports, "Outside of church circles, I find nowhere so much moral ferment as among corporation executives and teachers of business." Particularly in view of the development of nuclear weaponry, scientists have raised very serious questions about their moral responsibility. Doctors, lawyers, and homemakers are also asking important ethical questions. This enlarges the opening available to communication by the church. If now there is a greater readiness on the part of religious groups to give more concrete and secular content to theological generalizations, and if there is a greater readiness by vocational man to see the larger social and moral dimensions of his task, there should result an extremely fruitful dialogue.

This chapter attempts to focus religious resources on vocational dilemmas, not in terms of particular occupations, but in terms of areas for decision common to most occupations. Specific vocational groups such as farmers, salesmen, or university professors need in conversation together to explore choices which may be unique to themselves. General guidance can be given on defining issues and incorporating theological resources. Introducing such a religious dimension can be expected to make a distinct difference in several respects.

For one thing, a more transcendent orientation can sharpen our sensitivity about existing inadequacies. This would greatly increase the number of matters we consider to be loaded with moral significance. The kinds of problems considered by laymen as ethical are often quite limited, including elementary questions of honesty or of justice in person-to-person relationships. Even situations in these areas are far more complicated and ambiguous than is often realized. Honesty in business is considerably more than keeping one's hand out of the till or not cheating customers. Respect for persons goes considerably beyond matters of exploitative sex at office parties or discharging elderly breadwinners. Beyond such matters in-

volving single individuals or a limited range of moral principles lie other questions frequently neglected because they
are agonizingly complicated or because Christian practice
would go so far beyond prevailing standards. These might
include matters such as hiring and promotion policies for
Negroes, the morality of manufacturing armaments, or
the suitability of profit maximization as a motive. Many a
churchman has said that the range of morality does not
include technical decisions such as the kind of steel girders
necessary for safety in a bridge. Yet these matters also
affect persons or the use of God-given resources. Safety
for human life on a bridge is surely a matter of deep religious concern. To those who have eyes to see, every
choice they make during the working day in some way
affects their own growth or that of other persons and is
therefore to be made under God. All major choices deserve
time out for dedicated reflection.

Another form of sensitivity-training is the illumination
in depth provided by theological insight. For example,
denial of employment to racial minorities becomes a more
obvious evil when they are seen as sons of God about
whom he is particularly concerned because their need is
greater and the degree of their exploitation more serious.
Before making a decision, one should know what is actually going on. All that is going on is not always apparent
on the surface. When one is paying unskilled employees
the customary wage, one may not be aware of the number
of their children who cannot go to the college of their
choice. Jesus defined what is going on quite differently
than his hearers did. Those who saw themselves as merci-
ful or moral Jesus might describe as exploiters or hypo-
crites. They might see the issue as good relationships with
one's peers or as conformity to custom. Jesus was more
likely to see the issue as equal opportunity for all or as
conformity to divine standards never yet embodied in custom.

The Christian perspective enlarges the range of consequences considered relevant to decision, taking quite seri-

ously long-term and noneconomic results. The manufacture of lottery equipment or excessively luxurious items may produce profits and jobs. From a narrower economic perspective their production could then be justified. But a broader viewpoint might suggest that facilitating gambling encourages a "something for nothing" attitude which is detrimental to civilization. Or luxury items may be physically debilitating, or stimulate resentment in undeveloped countries, or exhaust natural resources to the deprivation of future generations. Such considerations would lead to the opposite conclusion. Their manufacture then is not justified.

As another major contribution, religious concern stimulates economic man to lengthen the list of options from which to choose. If he finds himself in a difficult dilemma in which apparently every possible move involves some evil, he is led more diligently to search out additional and unprecedented possibilities. For example, one of the more serious and often unrecognized problems of our time is planned obsolescence. This involves manufacturing products of a lower quality than might be made in order that they will wear out the sooner, and that their replacement will add up extra profits. Another almost unchallenged form is that of style change, causing discard of clothing or cars, not because they are worn out, but simply because they are outmoded. Both producers and consumers here easily become implicated in a prevailing immorality. Certainly these practices involve waste. Because their manufacture uses up resources of capital, time, and skill, we are not able to do other things which might contribute a great deal more to human welfare. Yet, if a producer does not engage in such practices to a certain extent, he may not be able to stay in business alongside less scrupulous competitors. If a consumer does not pay some attention to style, he may be dismissed by all his neighbors as a fanatic not worth listening to. Neither alternative is morally intriguing.

The person who understands his ethical obligation and

insists upon ingenuity in situations of ambiguity will considerably lengthen the list of options before him. Perhaps
he can only partially practice planned obsolescence. Or,
he may make a virtue of longevity and lack of model
changes, Volkswagen-style. Or he might appeal to legis-
latures for conservation laws to limit the drain on resources. Or a producer might initiate discussion by his
trade associations, hoping to find that other manufacturers
also reluctantly caught may join in an ethical code for the
industry. Or, at the same time that he does what seems
to be the best possible, he may also support educational
efforts, perhaps through the church, regarding the purpose
of material goods or the values of the simple life, in order
that consumer preferences might in the long run be
changed. Regardless of what his business policies need to
be, he might make the style of his private life a testimony
against conspicuous waste in consumption. Whatever the
form of his witness may be, a person is more ready to go
beyond his peers if he believes this to be the calling of
God. The initiative and courage to be the first in one's
field to try a morally more promising procedure is a product of religion at its best.

With these clues in mind, every man on his particular
job can find more creative ways to exert a constructive influence. With respect to each major troublesome decision,
he needs to focus sensitivity, clarify issues, broaden his
study of consequences, lengthen the list of possible options, and recall his highest loyalties. The layman, however, has a right to expect more help than these general
observations. To be sure, there is a level of specificity that
cannot be supplied by outsiders. Each man must work out
the details of his decision in his specific situation with
such help as he can gain from others in similar circumstances. But between the most general observations and
the day-to-day concrete details, possibly helpful comments
can be made about classes of choices that share some simi-
larities. There are at least three major areas for decision-

making which apply to all occupations. These involve relationships with other persons, the use of material goods, and questions concerning one's personal motivation.

The network of problems that grows out of interpersonal relationships is an extensive one. Decisions must be made with respect to others in the same occupation as business competitors, neighboring housewives, or other doctors. There are necessary relationships with subordinates or superiors in the same plant or office. Many have relationships with customers or suppliers, or with those in government or in other general social organizations that increasingly impinge on the world of work. In all these interpersonal situations typical problem areas tend to emerge, including telling the truth, protecting freedom, improving the quality of relationships, and doing justice.

The claim of truth can be an embarrassing one for the dynamic man of affairs. It requires that one's communication of meaning correspond with actual reality instead of conveying falsehood. An ethical man has been defined as a person who never goes back on his word—without first consulting his lawyer! A higher level of moral sensitivity would read considerably more than that into personal integrity! For example, what is the impeccably honest advertising man to do? The answer is especially hard when there are others in the field such as the cigarette copywriter who, untroubled by recent medical findings about smoking, said: "I'll take their money. I write for the man who feeds me." How does this differ from defenses made by the Nuremberg war criminals?

What is a contractor to do if his competitors falsify expected completion dates or descriptions of materials and thus continuously win the contracts? What is one to say about deceptively written guarantees or misleading packaging or oversimplified financial statements? Padded expense accounts may add to income but subtract from integrity. Yet there are situations, according to one engineer, in which a man must conform or his peers will turn against him. Even the most scrupulous among us may be questioned about the complete accuracy of references or recommendations that we write. Indeed, there is a serious ethical question whether one should reveal facts from a person's past that would be an obstacle to that person's employment, after the influence of those events has been completely eliminated. Which is the truer representation of the person? Or should parents tell young children all that they know about sex or about advanced nuclear physics? Should doctors reveal to dying patients their full prognosis in all cases? Even ministers have hidden, or given a false impression about some of their theological or social convictions in order to hold a job. In their defense it might be argued that if they did say all they believed on controversial issues, this would have an entirely different meaning to many of their hearers than it actually does to the minister, and therefore he would by his "honesty" be giving a false impression about himself. How many inaccuracies should journalists write into history? Should they ever suppress a story to please an advertiser? It could be argued that some misrepresentation is inevitable because all that occurs in a single day cannot possibly be printed. Whatever selection is made creates something of a false impression. Since it is the unusual that tends to be reported, it may easily appear that men bite dogs more often than dogs bite men.

Those who face any of these dilemmas had better be reminded of the importance of truth. Indeed, a man's "yes" should mean "yes" and his "no" should mean "no" (Matt. 5:37). A man's word should be better than his bond. Outer action and inner conviction ought to coincide. Those who easily break the truth are likely to be neglecting some of the consequences of their action. Trust and the continuation of a dependable social relationship depend on truth. Personal integrity is fundamental to all morality.

Just because we are concerned about protecting the truth, however, something like Bonhoeffer's chapter on truth in his *Ethics* should be required reading for every churchman. He successfully defends the proposition that the principle of telling the truth may require somewhat different forms of conduct in differing situations. As he put it, " 'Telling the truth', therefore, is not solely a matter of moral character; it is also a matter of correct appreciation of real situations and of serious reflection upon them." For example, the same word may convey a different meaning in the warmth of the family than it does in business or in public. Technical accuracy at one point may give a false impression at another point. To modify slightly one of Bonhoeffer's illustrations, if a teacher asked a child in class whether his father was a drunkard, to say "No" would be untrue if the father as a matter of fact was an alcoholic. But to say "Yes" would also give a false impression, arousing a popular picture of a "drunkard" in the minds of other children that did not at all coincide with this particular father's love and hard work. It is the total impression of the entire situation that should be as accurately conveyed as the circumstances allow. If a manufacturer has a better product than his competitors, at the same time that no one of them has a completely perfect product, he may not be able to give a simple "Yes" or "No" answer to the question, "Is your product 100 percent pure?" So long as his competitors are answering that question "Yes," he can scarcely say "No" without conveying the impression that his product is worse than those of his competitors. He must somehow find ways of conveying the truth that his is a purer product than others available. What should one say if, after a band of refugee Jews had passed by, a Nazi storm trooper rushed up to ask, "Have you seen the Jews?" To say "No" is a falsehood. If, on the other hand, a person says "Yes," he conveys the false impression that he does not care about the Jews and that he is ready to cooperate with the Nazi extermination policy.

This last illustration also reminds us that there are always other values than the one under consideration at

the moment. In addition to the claim of the truth, there
is also the claim of justice or concern for life. One often
has to decide which of two claims should be given priority. It is the fullest possible realization of a total system
of values that we ought to aim at. It is for this reason that
some extremely conscientious persons during Nazi days
began to forge passports and deliberately falsify information in order that the lives of the innocent might be saved.
There undoubtedly are similar situations on every man's
daily job. His problem is to protect the fullest measure of
truth which is consistent with the expression of a coherent
structure of values. On this matter there is no simple do-it-
yourself kit of ethical screwdrivers to adjust vocational
machinery. Yet the pressure is toward the most complete
and accurate representation that is possible. Under some
circumstances there may be hidden alternatives waiting to
be discovered. For example, careful interpretation or
imaginative statement may make possible both the preser-
vation of truth and other values. An adult, asked if a
relative was a drunkard, might competently go into the
details necessary to give a thoroughly accurate impression.
Sometimes it is possible to expose the fraud of dishonest
competitors. Or in addition to whatever immediate action
seems necessary one might embark on a long-term program
to train readers, listeners, or buyers to detect fallacies or to
test products. One can support programs such as those of
Better Business Bureaus or of the Federal Trade Commission or of consumers councils which try in some measure
to control economic fraudulence.

A second cluster of vocational dilemmas gathers around
the concept of freedom, in the sense of absence of external
restraint. All other things being equal, every man ought
to be allowed to act according to his own ideals instead
of being forced to compromise them in conformity with
pressures from outside himself. One of our great social
goals is that persons might become inner-directed participants in common decision rather than other-directed sub-

jects to dictatorial controls. In our vocational capacities
we repeatedly face questions of expressing such freedom
ourselves, or of creating the conditions under which other
persons may achieve liberty. For example, an employee
may be dissatisfied with the speed of work that has become
customary for the group to which he has been assigned.
He may be convinced that proper diligence in social contribution requires him to work faster. Yet if he is to hold
his job or retain his influence among fellow workers, he
must adapt to the existing standard which is enforced by
a variety of informal pressures. Subordinates continually
have to decide whether they will carry out policies of their
superiors even though they seriously disagree with them.
This involves a conflict between loyalty to employer and
obligation to the larger society. Even executives in all
kinds of organizations constantly face the possibility of
being asked to administer a group decision with which
they personally disagree.

Where does one draw the line against nonpersuasive
forms of pressure? What constitutes undue influence on
others? Many types of coercion seem inevitably involved
in economic life. Whenever there are scarce values such
as raw materials or capital or time to be assigned, somebody's hopes or plans must be frustrated. To what extent,
however, are we justified in adding to these inevitable
limitations on freedom? Are there any occasions on which
we ought to manipulate people as though they were
things? Certainly we should never be content with this
as a finally accepted pattern. Yet we do widely condone
paternalistic decisions. We honor the philanthropist. Well
we might, insofar as he has aided worthwhile causes. At
the same time, however, we overlook the fact that paternalistic philanthropy involves a unilateral decision which
controls others without their participation. When the
company decides, for example, that it is going to use a
surplus to build a workers recreation center rather than to
give them an increase in salary, it may be providing a

worthwhile facility but it is also denying the freedom of workers to dispose of the income that might have been theirs.

Collusion or price-rigging among competitors at the expense of consumers is widely frowned upon. But should salesmen provide gifts and entertainment (with or without call girls) for customers in order to influence their buying habits? Such adding of additional considerations that have nothing to do with the logical basis for choice is the essence of coercion. To what extent should anyone accept such gifts or kickbacks or bribes or payoffs? One politician described his policy on these matters by saying that he took nothing that could not be eaten or drunk at one sitting!

Great deeds can be done for liberty on the job as well as in politics. In our work relationships patterns of decision-making can be either democratic or autocratic. Citizens more often understand the importance of resisting dictatorial powers in government than they do the need for creating a free climate in the world of work. The freedoms of men include not only the right to speak and vote on affairs of state but also the fullest possible right to choose products, recreation, conditions of employment, or economic security. These latter matters are also basic to a free way of life. Every mature person can claim a vote on those matters which shape his development. Even when he is outvoted the sincere conscientious objector deserves such concessions to his scruples as will not endanger vital interests of the group. Just as sincere pacifists are given consideration by the state, so do conscientious minorities have some claim on business organizations. How can a chamber of commerce or a labor union or the American Medical Association protect the liberties of those who oppose a group position? How is it possible for a person to remain an autonomous and responsible individual in a large-scale economic organization?

At the same time that he asks for fullest possible

consideration, an objecting individual would have to admit that binding policy decisions must be made. It is not possible to grant absolute freedom to everyone. So long as we live in society the liberty of some must be restricted in order to protect the liberty of others. Each of us can repeat with appreciation, "Your freedom ends where my nose begins." Best possible action always means not absolutizing freedom but, rather, maximizing freedom. The best we can do is to provide the most possible liberty for the most possible persons. If majorities are to enjoy freedom, then minorities ordinarily must go along with democratically adopted policies.

Therefore, precisely because they believe in the greatest possible liberty, administrators or subordinates must often accept group decisions. They can demand only freedom to participate. On occasional matters that demand a greater compromise than they feel able to make, they have the alternative of resigning. When a man on the job faces this kind of decision he ought to weigh the comparative importance of other values involved, in addition to the grounds for his own objections to the majority decision. He might well also consider the flexibility of the situation. If it is likely to change in the foreseeable future, he should perhaps go along with the policy in the short run for the sake of contributing to longer-run changes. He might also try to anticipate the result of his own dramatic withdrawal. Is it likely to contribute to the positive witness he prefers, or may it actually have the opposite effect in leaving his point of view completely unrepresented in future decision-making?

The obligation to honor group decisions ordinarily is balanced by the democratic right to participate in such decisions. Whenever the power of those in the executive suites of corporations or labor unions or professional organizations or even churches denies such participation by the little man, then this power is to be called into question. It is increasingly clear that democracy has economic

as well as political significance. The emphasis on human
relations in industry has carried much of the same meaning. Now widely accepted as a sound business practice,
this includes management's listening to labor and providing procedures for fuller expression and participation
in decision. This implies recognition of representative
labor unions as well as internal democracy within those
unions. In neither case does this eliminate the executive's
right to full expression and active administration through
day-to-day decisions within the framework of the general
policy adopted by the group. In modern administration,
the trend is away from the old-fashioned chain of com-
mand with the man at the top making all major decisions
and barking out orders to be unquestioningly obeyed by
underlings. Now serious efforts are being made to tap
the skills and perspectives of many people through group
participation. Suggestions are actively solicited from the
lowliest worker, since his different segment of experience
may produce ideas that have dollar-and-cents value. Increasingly there is also a recognition of labor's right to
participate at the points at which it is most affected, beginning with wages and working conditions but now going
beyond those to a wider range of matters considered
suitable for collective bargaining.

This kind of approach involves a different attitude in
human relationships, whether in the family, the church,
the school, or the office. It goes beyond a desire to dominate by coercing compliance. Rather, it is an attitude of
genuine appreciation, of eagerness to learn from others,
and of accepting as normal equal participation by all those
properly concerned. All of us are egocentric enough that
it is hard to work out the practical gestures appropriate to
such an approach. One businessman, in a recent discussion group, pointed out that it is all very well to say that
"the man at the machine is king" and to invite his suggestions, but if his superiors do not actually listen to what the
man is saying, their dictatorial action belies their demo-

cratic words. The full implications of democracy have yet to be worked out in industry, the professions, and the family. Such experimentation is one of the more promising approaches toward a fuller expression of love in human community.

Christian insight into the quality of human relationships has broader implications than merely freedom. It calls for the genuine fellowship that provides an enabling environment for the realization of authentic personhood under God. The recognition that all men are made in the image of God eliminates the possibility that any man shall be regarded as a mere functionary or as a "hand" to be used by the "boss." We often seem to care for machines and use persons instead of loving persons and using machines. If we see others as God sees them, we will know that every man deserves attention and respect.

This kind of "level look" toward others makes it easier to learn to work together in the full dimensions of cooperation. Paul may have been speaking of the comradeship of the church when he referred to our being as hands and eyes to each other, but this is also a goal for a more inclusive society. It is better that men should work together for common ends than that they should struggle antagonistically for diverse ends.

Again such ethical imperatives underscore the problems that proliferate in vocational life. An individual may find himself in an organization in which it is all too common to undercut associates. Should he also make his peers appear in a bad light in order to be more likely to get a promotion himself? Cliques, behind-the-scenes maneuvering, and intraorganizational politics often give point to the saying, "It isn't what you know, but who you know." The impersonal contacts which characterize large organizations make it difficult to maintain the friendly relationships necessary to social life at its best. Men who feel anonymous in a large group or who can hide behind a faceless corporation often do such villainy as they would never attempt as individuals. In a discussion group of bankers, one of them asked, "Could Jesus Christ have been a good banker?" An officer in one of the nation's largest banks replied, "Yes, I suppose so—in a small town." It would be interesting to hear a small-town banker's reply, particularly in these days of branch banking.

In relationships between persons who are in the same business, where does unfair competition start? What about price wars or industrial espionage or hiring a knowledge-able employee away from a competitor? In relationships with labor unions, should one adopt the stance of cold war or of problem-solving? In relationships among workers, the human equation on the production line makes a difference in output and quality. A relief man may get angry because an assembly worker takes too long on his relief, and walk off the line before the assembler returns. A worker may take revenge on the foreman by sabotaging the job. Those who feel no recognition may cause trouble just to let their superiors know that they are there.

In all human relationships, a healthy realism is always in order. If we see men as they are, we will recognize the necessity for some rivalry or conflict. The spur of competition is usually necessary to maintain the highest efficiency. Some conflict results if different alternatives are presented in discussion. Progress requires such vigorous competition between ideas. The hope for continuous affability and placid harmony is not only naïve but also mistaken. The problem is to keep competition and conflict from becoming extreme or self-defeating. When it becomes cynical or cutthroat, it brings out the worst in both parties.

The Christian view of man also provides a basis for humility, openness, appreciation, and support. Seeing another as a center of worth makes it easier to listen to his deepest questions and harder to overwhelm him by fili-buster. We will be more considerate as we realize that every man we meet is fighting a terrific inner battle. If we begin to love others as God loves us, it becomes our goal also that they shall find fulfillment. We can then come to realize a little of what it means for free men to communicate without fear and mistrust, and for altruistic men to become servants to each other. It is in this direction in which the Christian always leans. Institutional machinery may impose grave resistance, but the individual operators of the machinery can to a certain extent lubricate the gears by their individual style of life.

Another major complex of vocational dilemmas clusters around the concept of justice. These are problems that have to do with the distribution of the products of industry or the values of work. Who is to get what? If each ought to receive his due, how are such proper shares to be determined? Sylvia and Benjamin Selekman have spoken of the constant dilemma involving "the technical 'must' against the ethical 'ought.'" What one has to do to meet the requirements of business efficiency may be quite different from what one wants to do in order to be socially just. It is desirable to do the right thing by each individual person and group within the firm, but it is also necessary to make a success of the enterprise for the sake of workers and consumers in general, or for larger social ends.

The problem of distributive justice is raised in the question of how the product of industry is to be distributed. When there is a surplus, should it go primarily to the stockholders, or to workers, or to consumers in the form of lower prices? In a survey of business opinion reported in the *Harvard Business Review* for July–August, 1961, five out of six executives agreed with the statement, "For corporation executives to act in the interest of shareholders alone, and not also in the interest of employees and consumers, is unethical." How is this to be translated into percentages going to each group?

Or, in cases of discipline and discharge, what is justice?

For example, should older employees be retained because
of their long service and their unusual need? Or, should
they be discharged because they are less able and therefore increase costs? Is favoritism toward relatives or friends
ever justifiable in employment and promotion? What
should be the basis for medical or legal fees? Is income of
the client to be considered, or simply service performed?
What is a just price policy? Is discrimination in favor of
"price buyers" justifiable when other loyal customers are
not treated the same?

Numerous forms of conflicts of interests are troublesome for a variety of occupations. Should one use favored
information for personal advantage? If an individual's
company is about to merge and he has reason to believe
that the public announcement will drive its stock up,
should he buy stock for himself? Should he tell his friends
or his broker? Or is it ethical to oversell customers? Should
a lawyer ever "take the client for a ride," going to trial
with a case that cannot be won? Should he attempt to
reconcile couples or take the divorce business plus the fee?
Most of us have to make decisions about distributing the
services we render. Should the politician represent the "interests" that can contribute to his campaign, or should he
represent the "little people"? How much time should a
mother spend with her children and how much in community causes? How much more attention should a teacher
give to pupils who have special needs, to the detriment
of others? In a group focused on the ethics of trade unions,
a labor leader once asked whether he should advise a local
to accept a contract that was not the best that might have
been secured. In return for accepting this somewhat easier
contract, the same employer had offered to allow the
union to organize another of his plants in a different state.
It was not a simple problem, because the union was genuinely concerned about the welfare of the workers in the
other state as well as in the existing local union. Should
one serve more persons not quite so well, or fewer persons

better? This sometimes has international ramifications. Is it right for an industry to demand a tariff to protect its profit and its workers' wages, but at the expense of a foreign producer and population?

The procedure for making decisions on all such matters can be illustrated in a case from one of the discussion outlines of the Detroit Industrial Mission. It deals with one of our most urgent problems of justice, the hiring and upgrading of members of racial minorities. A particular department has a two weeks' deadline for developing data to present to the top policy committee of the corporation in support of a new program which holds great promise for public service. With good morale the members of the department are working maximum overtime hours as the only way to meet the deadline. Then a key analyst is called to another state for his father's funeral and resigns to accept a key position in his family's business. In reply to an urgent request for an immediate replacement, the personnel department recommends as the most promising candidate a young Negro. He has a pleasant personality, is well trained, can undoubtedly do the job, and the company has a fair-employment policy. The difficulty is that two other analysts with whom he would have to work most closely are bitterly prejudiced against Negroes. Given time, the matter might be worked out. But the deadline is only two weeks away.

In cases such as this, there is no simple calculus for mathematically weighing the alternatives. The consequences are often unpredictable. One can deal only with probabilities. Yet there is still the obligation to do the best one can. Each decision must be individualized. Much depends in our illustration on how deeply prejudiced the two possible objectors are, on the kinds of responses they are likely to make to various approaches, and on how socially important the new program is.

Decisions in distributive justice require weighing rival claims. Mere desire or greed is no strong support for a demand. In a world of finite men we must take into account what persons deserve to get in the light of their previous contribution. Some extra payment for extra work is necessary to keep partially egoistic men working at their best. Yet, from the Christian perspective, more important than greed or deed is need. A priority is to be given to the disprivileged, those who have suffered past exploitation and often yet have no one to speak for them. Biblical concern for the poor is of this sort. The good Samaritan did not check the victim's references or employment record. Unusual need in itself constitutes a superior claim.

In adding up considerations on the two sides, we are often forced to compare dissimilar values, like adding apples and oranges. In the illustration, how much unemployment for the Negro equals how much new service by the company? One help here is the concept of a hierarchy of values discussed in the previous chapter. Residents of California and Florida might consider oranges to be twice as important as apples. All of us should consider moral or religious growth to have priority over any simple accumulation of physical values that was not significantly related to such higher growth.

Also, one should try to list the full range of consequences for any decision. It is not only a matter of unemployment for the Negro, but there are other serious social losses resulting from continued racial discrimination. These losses include domestic riots or increased influence for Communists in Africa. There is always also a future dimension to outcomes. We should comparatively favor those persons or policies most likely to make the greatest contribution to social need during the years ahead.

Before making a decision between two claims, we ought always to exhaust our imaginative ingenuity in a search for any possible option that might satisfy both claims. Could the Negro be employed in another department and later be transferred in after more adequate preparation? Or is the notion of preparing the way a mistaken one, and is the best possibility of acceptance simply employing him without any fanfare? Or could one go to the two prejudiced people with a full sharing of the dilemma, asking their cooperation?

After the situation has been individualized, claims compared in the light of their full consequences, and the list of alternatives lengthened, that choice is finally necessary which seems to maximize values. Even worse than a decision that is something less than perfect is to avoid responsibility for decision entirely. There is no substitute for an act of courageous faith based on the most careful analysis possible. Everyone will make some mistakes, but as a union leader once said in a vocational discussion group, he can always hope he will not make three mistakes in a row lest they become a habit!

Another major category of vocational perplexities relates to the use of material goods. The physical assets of life have always been a concern to the Christian community because the world of nature was seen as the creation of God. It was a trust granted to man to be used with a sense of stewardship. Man's management of material things was to be for the purposes of God.

Material things, therefore, are to be looked upon as good. They embody genuine value, though it is always only instrumental and subordinate value. They gain their significance because they contribute to higher ends. The fruit of the soil and the resources of the earth can become foundation stones upon which are built the social, moral, and spiritual values of life. The latter values are to be placed ahead of material values. The use of the luxuries of a rich universe is to be directed not toward self-indulgence but to social welfare.

Such a view of the purposes of physical creation lays upon us a double obligation. In addition to employing material resources toward proper ends, we also have a duty to develop competence. We are to manage material resources well, becoming capable, conscientious, and diligent workmen. A teacher who works with children always deals in futures and therefore needs to develop excellent teaching methods. The doctor needs to be a good doctor. But his is not the only skill upon which life may depend. Lives may be terminated also by the poor products of industry. The successful businessman is partly judged by the profitability of his production. He can provide no service through his business unless he stays in business. He must ensure a greater output than input if he is to continue to deliver his products. The concept of efficiency, however, must now be brought to include also social efficiency. A successful businessman is the one who best provides what human life requires. Regardless of what a person's vocation is, if he announces himself as a particular kind of worker and cannot do the job, he is perpetrating a fraud. Christian vocation requires more than professional skill; it can be content with nothing less.

Such a discussion raises questions about production and sales policies as they affect quality of product and conservation of resources. Conscientious craftsmen should stand aghast at low-quality goods and shoddy workmanship. What inferior materials, for example, should never be used by the electrician or plumber even when he feels great pressure to cut costs? In manufacturing there is often a conflict between quantity and quality. One plant making air conditioners ran out of four-inch mounting bolts. The solution was, "Then use three-inch bolts, but get out 200 units by 3:30." What if a few months later in another city a unit comes loose from its mounting and falls on someone below? Should a person ever settle for mediocrity, a "C" average, when he could be producing superior services? An advertiser, for example, may feel that he should sponsor a high-quality television show to elevate public taste, but stockholders would not then get maximum advertising coverage for their dollar. Answers to all these questions undoubtedly involve some flexibility in order to protect larger values. They also require building a platform below which one will not fall.

Another moral pitfall in the use of material goods is waste. Each time natural resources or human energy are diverted from their intended purpose, God's creation is raped or despoiled. All of us are caught in the cultural standards of our time which encourage wasteful affluence. We buy more than we need and truck the excess garbage or refuse to the city dump. The housewife deciding on how many cans of root beer to buy, or her husband assenting to an early replacement of the living room rug, are both handling sacred things, the product of God's creation. We might well ask about the relationship of most of our television and newspaper advertising to the principle "Thou shalt not covet."

How much cake should a Christian enjoy while there are millions in the world who lack bread? We cannot decide this simply by keeping up with the expectations of our peers, nor is it good enough simply to buy anything that we want and can afford. The concept of stewardship leads us to direct all our resources toward the greatest human need, for that is surely the purpose of God. If young men in India need college dormitory rooms more than we need a mountain cottage, we ought to send the money to India. In the modern world with massive poverty in undeveloped areas, this would seem to lead us to send all that we have. There apparently is always a greater social need elsewhere. Perhaps we ought to balance this insight with another principle—or is this rationalization? God also calls us to become stewards of our abilities and energies. Therefore, it might be argued that we can spend on ourselves whatever is necessary for effectiveness in our calling. This would mean enough calories to sustain energy but not much whipped cream. This would allow dependable transportation but not extra chrome on the car. In an affluent society this might require a somewhat higher standard than simple necessities if we are to have any influence in our generation. Otherwise, whatever message we speak might be dismissed as the word of an unreliable fanatic. But, on the other hand, if we completely duplicate the standard of those about us, we can speak no effective word either, for it is then completely contradicted by our actions.

Perhaps this leads to a standard of living that might be described by the phrase "functional simplicity"—a style of consumption cut to essentials, but with a purpose, to fulfill the functions of love. Even in a moderated form this still remains a revolutionary concept. If a person keeps the tension tight with his religious ideals, he will be here challenging contemporary consumer practice, as well as defining the purpose of production differently.

Another set of dilemmas clusters around the production of what might be called social "illth" instead of wealth. Supplying goods or services that are socially undesirable quite clearly cannot be accepted as a vocational goal. The significance of material goods lies in their use toward a higher end. They are to be used to overcome poverty, drudgery, inequality, meaninglessness, and not to increase the sum total of destruction, enslavement, and despair. Nevertheless, there are complicated questions connected with this insight. If a man is convinced that cigarettes are dangerous, should he grow tobacco if that is the best way to feed his family? Should a scholar in the university ever use his abilities in what he considers irrelevant study so long as there is a demand for it, either by the administration or by outside employers? Is a banker responsible for the kind of production that results from his loans? Should he consider social consequences as well as safety in a particular investment? Is a research scientist responsible for the destructive uses to which his work is put? Or does he make a distinction between basic research and applied technology, leaving responsibility for the latter to others? Should an artist ever paint what will sell instead of what his inner being demands? Or does he have an obligation to use canvas and pigments in ways that reflect humility, respect for objects, and a sense of mystery and deeper meaning? In other words, is he always to paint religiously, somehow revealing the presence of God in nature and life? Only when the emphasis is placed there does any occupation become a calling.

This is closely connected with the issue of personal motivation on the job. Is one's primary drive egoistic or altruistic? Do workers live only for payday, or do they have a higher purpose? Are power, privilege, and wealth to be used for private or public ends? Selfishness may be expressed not only as greed but also as anger, fear, pride, desire for revenge, or lust for power. In any of these forms selfishness is self-defeating rebellion against God. It blocks personal growth and destroys community. Christian love involves radical expressions of altruism. This is the secret of meaningful existence which rescues us from the desolation of nonpurpose. Yet no one of us completely lives this way. Our motives are always so badly mixed that they might be called homogenized.

Is personal profit ever justifiable? The answer to that can be summarized in the formula: never as basic motivation, frequently as necessary means for service. This is to say that the fundamental drive of the Christian is not to serve himself, but that certain returns to the self make one better able to act altruistically toward others. A higher salary allows a college education or books to study; a profit in business is necessary to finance the function it exists to perform. The problem is to keep regarding the personal enhancement always as means and never as end. Paul Ramsey has put this well by saying, "No more disastrous mistake can be made than to admit self-love onto the ground-floor of Christian ethics as a basic part of Christian obligation, however much concern for self-improvement, for example, may later come to be a secondary, though entirely essential, aspect of Christian vocation." It should be noted that this cannot be turned into a general argument for profit maximization. It is a justification only for a satisfactory profit, whatever is necessary to contribute to social goals. A man is never to sell his soul for his salary; he is simply to accept the salary essential to service.

This leads us to probe more deeply into our theology of

work. To what ends do the wheels of industry go around? What is the purpose of our labor? One historical interpretation is that work is to be regarded as punishment. Because Adam and Eve ate of the forbidden fruit, they were condemned to earn bread by the sweat of their brow. Labor became a curse to be endured. Parents may even yet unintentionally transmit this attitude to their children when they complain about the rigors of the day's work. Or work has been regarded as either penance or prevention of sin. By arduous toil man might think of himself as working out the penalties for his misdoing, or he might be avoiding mischief by disciplined busyness.

None of these is an adequate Christian view. Work ought to be regarded rather as participation in the creative purposes of God. It is positive opportunity. Civilization is the outcome of labor, and personal meaning is found in joyous toil. God works and we are his coworkers (John 5:17; I Cor. 3:9). This is the emphasis of the traditional Protestant concept of vocation. The labor of the Christian is more than mere activity. His is to be a purposeful disciplined exertion, an answer to the summons of God to continue his creation. It is a collective venture to transform the world.

Not all available work fits the category of response to God. A fair amount of what we call employment today is service of various devils. Many early Christians for a time refused to enter a lengthy list of occupations that they felt were related to a pagan society. Equally sensitive spirits today might draw the line at a longer list of banned occupations than might at first be realized. Not only occupations that were plainly destructive would be excluded, but also those which uselessly wasted resources or which contributed primarily to the perpetuation of an exploitative system.

Taking the divine calling seriously would decisively affect one's choice of a vocation. The basic distinction to be made is not between so-called sacred or secular occupations, or between those occupying different social-status levels. The choice is to be made by comparing personal capacities, interests, and backgrounds with the hierarchy of need in the contemporary world. Each man needs to make clear who he is. As a person with particular abilities he looks for the place he belongs in terms of social priorities. Does the world need bigger and better bombs more than it needs air purification, getting radioactivity and industrial garbage out of the atmosphere? Is it better to explore the resources of the moon or to eliminate poverty on the earth? The person intent upon uncommon creativity would weigh differently some of the tests usually used in vocational guidance. Those social needs would loom larger which were more fundamental or more urgent or less attended to by others. The fundamental question would become, "At what point can a person with my interests and abilities contribute most significantly to the greatest human need?"

Within any vocation a particular job is to be chosen, involving a specific employer or specialization or product. A schoolteacher may feel called to teach in the slum rather than in the wealthy suburb. Others may equally be called to a mission to the successful. Engineers or stenographers might refuse higher salary offers in order to join enterprises more genuinely devoted to the welfare of people. William Stringfellow began by practicing law in Harlem. A vice-president of General Electric Company, slated to succeed the president, is reported to have resigned his position because, in his words, "I began to realize I was serving no socially worthwhile purpose in helping a giant to become even bigger."

Within any particular job an individual faces a choice of style of work. Of the many aspects of any job description, which does he choose to emphasize? It is not only a question of "Where do I work?" but also a question of "How do I work?" Anyone who sees his work as a part of God's campaign is likely to do it more thoroughly and energetically, and with greater stress on its most creative aspects. A mother in the home needs to decide comparatively how much time to give to the children and what activities to include in those children's hours. A teacher can often speed up her paper work somewhat in order to do more counseling. Or she needs to decide whether to place more emphasis on transmitting knowledge or on nurturing personality. Albert Schweitzer has pointed out that reverence for life makes a vocational difference because "it demands of all a portion of their life for their fellows." All workers face the question of whether to indulge in those aspects of a job which increase personal comfort, or in those portions through which they may win some victory for humanity.

These issues can be faced within realistic limits. Not all desired jobs are obtainable. Every job has some comparatively useless requirements. Work needs therefore to be directed both by love and by wisdom. The religious person must fuse his faith and the facts, or in Paul Ramsey's phrase, he must act in terms of "enlightened unselfishness." Yet even in the worst manifestations of the human predicament there is ordinarily a range of options open. The worker can avoid the grosser expressions of egoism; he does not need to drop down to running in the rat race for vastly unequal profit or dictatorial power or undeserved prestige. He can push to the point of greatest service under existing conditions. Or, if it is impossible to hold an existing job without too great exploitation of others, a person can often change jobs. Many have found it helpful to have a like-minded group review their motivation and its manifestations. Discussion among Christians in the same occupation can unearth novel creative possibilities.

There is the further problem of protecting the conscientious enterpriser and society as a whole against those with the most grossly egoistic motivation. This may require legislation to safeguard decent business practices and consumer standards. Examples might be food and drug laws, securities and exchange regulation, highly progressive income taxes, or antitrust laws. Or we might encourage the development of professional codes of ethics for self-policing by those in an occupation. Some use is now being made of commissions of citizens or tripartite councils on which the public is represented to advise business and labor on the social consequences of particular acts. Or, certain members might be appointed to boards of directors as watchdogs for the public, even as consumer counselors are now appearing in government. A social audit of business and the professions becomes as important as an economic audit. One can often help to greater success those individuals who are more altruistic by patronizing them, by promoting them to more influential positions, or by voting for them for office. Underlying whatever else we do is the need to develop more effective, modernized programs of evangelism, to confront all men with the power of the Christian faith to transform basic motivations and to multiply the numbers of those who look upon their work as ministry.

In facing the variety of dilemmas that have been discussed in this chapter, Christian ethics provides not a detailed code in which we mechanically look up a problem in the index and find the matching prescription already fully worked out. It provides, rather, a general orientation growing out of the accumulated wisdom of the past which points directions for the future. It is a dynamic way of life which, within these guidelines, keeps us working out new responses to novel situations. The moral guidance of religious faith comes to us, not in an unreal world of utopian perfection, but in the present world where men sweat and struggle. God does not now expect perfect outcomes. He asks us to do the best we can with the resources we have.

Luther's doctrine of masks suggests that God always veils his presence. We can see him behind the outward appearance of the world of nature. He is in the housewife, the scientist, the worker. God can influence the world by our day-to-day decisions, by the quality and direction of our vocations. Whether it be carpenters who are primarily concerned about building houses for families, or scientists unlocking the potentialities of nature, or administrators more concerned about creativity than custom—in all these ways workers affect the fundamental character of culture. In this mission on weekdays we can be either morally slovenly or morally heroic. If we seriously ask what God is working at in our place of work, and what he therefore proposes that we do, we are the more likely to show some signs of heroism.

4

Creative Citizenship
in the Community

A MORT GERBERG cartoon, reproduced by Marshall McLuhon and Quentin Fiore in *The Medium Is the Massage,* shows a mod mother reading to her child. From a "Dick and Jane" primer of the future she is quoting: " 'See Dick. See Dick protest. Protest, Dick! Protest!' " Before this text is used with first-graders each of us might like to draw the accompanying illustration to show a type of protest he finds acceptable! Even so, most of us agree that society would be safer if children were brought up from even earlier than primer days with a sense of social responsibility. No democracy is healthy unless its people as a matter of course protest evil, while they also speak, vote, and act in defense of justice.

Personages of the past won a place in history books because they pledged lives, honor, and fortunes to difficult demands of freedom and righteousness. This is still one avenue to the newspapers or the history texts, but now an individual can also be favorably reported and achieve high status for being the best-dressed or the most dramatically hedonistic playboy. In an affluent society idleness and pleasure without accompanying responsibility become a realistically possible way of life for the masses. The set of life values associated with the international jet set does not conspicuously include spending time working for the United Nations or progressive legislation at the state capital. In less extreme forms, the bankruptcy of banality is

73

also illustrated by the prominence currently given to hobbies. Recreation is essential to creativity, but spending too much time on canasta while bombs hang over our heads becomes personally debilitating and socially destructive. Many club activities are tired, trite patterns which no longer match modern facts. Gibson Winter refers to the "mass amnesia" of the suburb, a fashionable forgetfulness by which we shut out the grim realities of the world.

For all age groups this flight from any reminder of unpleasant obligations must be replaced by competence in caring. A young person whose future is being charted by the decision of his elders is rightly determined to have something to say. A young parent whose children's lives are at stake should insist that the world be made safe for children. A modern woman who finds household tasks unsatisfying in her home with more laborsaving devices and fewer functions performed by the family unit may find significance in wider participation in civic life. Somewhat older persons whose children have left home and whose incomes are now high enough to allow some flexibility of choice bring particular resources to community-building. Those who have reached the peak of their careers and have had to come to terms with the fact that they will never be President of the United States or of their corporation can still extend the range of their usefulness in society. Even retired persons do not need to lay down civic participation at the time they give up their vocational jobs. Senior citizens, who still need to be needed, constitute a large unused reservoir of manpower with greatly expanded leisure. For all these persons, definition of the socially acceptable "thing to do," which already includes owning a car or learning to read and write, should also come to include personal strategy for citizenship in the community. Fortunately, a rich assortment of procedures is available even to the common man.

One major avenue of action open to every normal person is talk. For anyone interested in social change, "Talk it up" is sound advice. This is a way of "gossiping the gospel," to use a phrase coined in the East Harlem Protestant Parish. Public opinion is to a considerable extent formed by face-to-face verbalization, and in the last analysis public opinion still wields the scepter in a democracy. Even in a dictatorship, suppression and propaganda are unconscious compliments paid by despotic rulers to the power of mass opinion. In spite of the apathy of many citizens, or the disproportionate power of a few, or the imperfect correspondence between the actions of representatives and the wishes of the people, no major public policy is permanently possible without at least the silent acquiescence of most of the citizenry. As Thomas A. Bailey has pointed out in his study of public opinion, "If Mr. Average American wants to get a glimpse at the power behind the officeholder's chair, all he has to do is pick up a mirror and look into it."

While high-powered publicity plays a part in molding the popular mind, studies show that informal conversational contacts are amazingly potent. Lazarsfeld, Berelson, and Gaudet found that during the 1940 election, "on an average day, at least 10% more people participated in discussions about the election—either actively or passively—than listened to a major speech or read about campaign items in a newspaper." These political conversations were also more likely to reach those people who had not already made up their minds. Personal contacts have certain psychological advantages. They are more casual and nonpurposive, less selected by the listener, and more adaptable to individual reactions. They are reinforced by trust in an intimate from one's own status group, by personal loyalty, and by more immediate rewards for compliance. People can change people better than more impersonal media can.

Lazarsfeld and his associates called those persons who were most concerned and articulate about issues the "opinion leaders." These amateur architects of public opinion were found not to be identical with the most socially prominent or the wealthiest citizens. On the contrary, they were found in all occupational groups in somewhat the same proportions. Workers in the factories, professional persons in their offices, housewives who hold teas —all of these can help to elect presidents or to declare wars. Everyone of us has repeated opportunities for such social influence in varied informal groups. Forums constantly take place around firesides as friends discuss significant topics. The contribution of a home to its community is partially measured by the conversation that flows around its dinner table. A secretary can raise the significance of coffee-break chatter. A remark in a barbershop may intensify prejudice, while the denial of a false rumor increases tolerance and understanding.

If we are to project ideas through the common currency of conversation, we had better keep small talk introductory. Such topics have rapport value in that they get us off on common ground, but they scarcely compound public intelligence regarding war or poverty. Why should we spend much time discussing the weather, about which we can do nothing, when we could talk of world peace, about which we can do something? Conversation has a fellowship function. There are times for relaxation and recreation. Yet, if the typical hostess were to record and play back the dinner conversation of her guests, the experience might cause considerable consternation among thoughtful people. It is possible to be extremely vocal without being vital.

Informal conversation as a type of interpersonal communication can be supplemented by organizing more formal discussion opportunities, such as classes, forums, conferences, or workshops. The groups to which one already belongs may be ready-made discussion groups; they constantly talk about something. The subject might just as well be socially significant. Deputation teams, caravans, or speakers bureaus can be organized. Radio or television broadcasts are sometimes possible. All of these contribute to that incessant interaction of minds out of which creative social solutions come.

A widespread ferment of popular discussion is one way to balance the disproportionate power of small elites. During a British general election campaign I once saw a poster on the bulletin board of a London university which might have reflected stereotypes held by any party. Convinced of the comparative poverty of their party, students were recruiting workers for inexpensive house-to-house canvassing. The slogan on the poster was, "Let our enthusiasm make up for their limousines!" If democracy is to function soundly, the energy of the little people and the activity of vital interest groups at the grass roots must match the public relations funds of powerful minority interests.

In addition to being intelligently vocal, a solitary citizen with a concern can write. Like conversation, correspondence with friends can be entirely devoted to yesterday's rain and tomorrow night's movie, or it can include a discussion of important problems. If our letters are to give an accurate picture of ourselves, they ought to become vehicles for sharing our thinking on current issues. In correspondence with persons at a distance, our pens or typewriters become amplifiers for our voices.

Periodically, letters need to be directed to key persons in the community, such as educators, corporation executives, labor leaders, or association officers. Vance Packard in *The Waste Makers* pointed out that since consumers' letters to giant corporations are few, executives tend to overreact. With some exaggeration, he observed: "One strong letter . . . can create concern in the executive suite. . . . Two letters of protest will create panic. Three letters of protest will create pandemonium."

Editors of newspapers and magazines are important people to correspond with, especially if they control "Letters to the Editor" columns. A letter published there may be more widely read than the newspaper's own editorials. When a person has a letter printed in a major paper, he is probably speaking to the largest audience that he will ever address. To help your missive reach the presses instead of the wastebasket, keep it short, make only one or two interesting points, and try to relate it to a recent editorial or article. Those with some experience in such matters also suggest writing while an issue is timely or newsworthy. Type, if possible, double-spacing, and on only one side of the paper. Use simple words, short sentences, avoid abuse, and include supporting facts or a relevant personal experience. Whenever writing to several papers in the same city, change the contents sufficiently to give each paper an original letter. Do not be discouraged if many of your letters are not printed. Do not overlook smaller, local papers where competition for space may not be so keen.

Closely related to personal correspondence is the distribution of literature as a sort of extension of one's remarks through the writings of others. Occasionally, leaflets can be enclosed in letters. Posters on bulletin boards, exhibits in store windows, or displays on literature tables have unrealized possibilities for the person of imagination. Well-selected materials can be distributed at strategic times and places, such as at meetings, before or after church, or through the mail. Or a person may become a one-man book-of-the-month club, occasionally buying a significant book which he then lends to others. A footnote to the Scriptures might have said, "Do not hide your books under a bushel." As the early circuit riders carried bulging saddlebags of literature through the geographical wilderness, we can scatter organizing ideas in print through the ideological confusion.

The testimony of our individual actions is also an extension of our words. To witness to their beliefs, Old Testament prophets named their children in ways that carried the desired message. Whether or not we participate actively in community organizations transmits a message to all who know us. Every person witnesses to his neighbors on Sunday morning, depending on whether or not he drives to church or works on the lawn. We may buy luxurious homes or expensive clothes, not realizing that this is also advertising our priorities in a world in want. All such nonverbal communication becomes a kind of propaganda of the deed, a petition by performance.

In addition to interpersonal communication, effective witness in the community requires joining and becoming active in organized groups. Over a century ago De Tocqueville wrote: "Among democratic nations, . . . all the citizens are independent and feeble; they can do hardly anything by themselves. . . . They all, therefore, become powerless if they do not learn voluntarily to help one another. . . . As soon as several of the inhabitants of the United States have taken up an opinion or a feeling which they wish to promote in the world, they look out for mutual assistance; and as soon as they have found one another out, they combine. From that moment they are no longer isolated men, but a power seen from afar, whose actions serve for an example and whose language is listened to."

Action through groups has now become even more necessary than it was in former days. Decisions in mass society are made by interaction between groups rather than by individual confrontation in some sort of town meeting. Morality must now prove adequate to a situation in which we deal more with strangers than with friends, in which our contacts are more often casual than intimate. In a specialized urban society we cannot give personal service to all those in need. To live the altruistic life we must affiliate with organizations.

Furthermore, our mass society is characterized by great aggregations of power. How does a person influence the business community or bureaucratic government, or organized social agencies, or even school systems, as a lone individual? For the average person the answer is, not at all. But if he joins with others, he compounds strength to a realistic level. A united impact is stronger and a strategy jointly planned is likely to be sounder. Joining one's allies is as necessary for effectiveness in large populations as elevators are in skyscrapers. If no one else becomes interested, a project does not survive its initiator. One solution to the problem of the little man in big society is democratic participation in vital interest groups.

Not only is cooperation a prerequisite for social action; it is also an important means for personal growth. The power of the Spirit is released within the worshiping, serving fellowship. Also in groups other than the church come sounder guidance and deeper insight than any single member would consistently have. The group increases one's sense of security in meeting unaccustomed hazards and one's persistence against opposition. Group support releases capabilities and provides resources that members may never have known to exist. One woman, after she had stood up in a neighborhood meeting to defend the rights of a Negro couple who had recently moved in, said, "I lost a whole set of friends today and gained a whole new set, and I like my new friends much better."

Even in the smallest communities, some kindred spirits can usually be found, persons who may have been silent because they too felt they were alone. One's husband or wife is a strong beginning. A first responsibility is to provide for children the kind of experiences and parental example which will nurture community builders. Outside the home, a high school teacher, a laborer who enjoys reading, or other unsuspected persons may prove to be like-minded. Especially in larger communities there are probably organizations existing already in the area of one's concern. These may include vocational groups (such as labor unions, the Chamber of Commerce, or the American Medical Association), social-welfare groups (such as the Parent-Teachers' Association or Community Chest), or social-reform groups (such as the United Nations Association or the National Association for the Advancement of Colored People).

The church has a unique claim for support. As the conserver of the highest insights from the past it also becomes the conscience of contemporary society. It confronts men with the will of God. It leads men to vital contact with the power of God. It specializes in those ethical and religious matters which are the most basic elements in any social philosophy. As an institution it carries a considerable amount of prestige in the public mind. It has the resources that are necessary for widespread and rapid change—a meeting place in every village and neighborhood in the country, a sizable body of consecrated members, professionally trained leaders, and ready-made educational groups. Its comparative independence from entangling alliances or reactionary pressures has often left it more free for progressive leadership than any other agency. Any religiously motivated, socially concerned person might well begin with affiliation with the church.

It is also true that he ought not end there. Other promising groups also demand support. The church can have too rich a program, absorbing the energy of its members in attending meetings in the sanctuary and postponing or eliminating their witness in the world. Even too detailed Bible study or prolonged personal-growth groups may monopolize time at the expense of social expression. In education or group therapy we may polish interpersonal relationships to a high gloss and leave intergroup relationships filthy and abrasive. This is passing the point of diminishing returns in activity within the church, while we could still gain larger increasing returns in the community.

Just as a person joins the church, he should join at least one community group working for brotherhood or justice, not as a diversion from his church but as an extension of the work of the church. The church ought to recruit its members for such selected community agencies. Sending representatives of the church to a city council meeting is the equivalent of sending out disciples two by two to carry the gospel. When a man gives his full energy to making the policy of his company more socially responsible, he might well be excused from office-holding in the church. He can probably do more for equal employment opportunities as vice-president of a large company than as chairman of the social-action committee of his congregation.

To be sure, the most suitable organizations must be selected from among the many appealing for support. All kinds of clever power movements may wear the garments of rationality and goodwill, while in actuality they represent private interest and ineffectual procedures. Among the tests to be applied to groups is that of consistency with one's own ideals. While a measure of compromise is necessary in any united action, one cannot achieve one's ends through channels that run in contrary directions. Does the group operate democratically? Are its purposes and its methods in accord with my ethical convictions? Can I have confidence in its general membership and in its constitutional procedures? Certainly one needs to avoid groups with totalitarian ties, whether on the right or on the left. A second set of questions relates to practical effectiveness. How realistic is the program of a particular group? What is its potential promise in comparison with other organizations in the field? How does it relate to the most strategic points for attack under current conditions? A long list of reputable organizations operating in various areas will meet these tests. There is no reason for not showing up at a selected meeting and beginning to work.

In planning group affiliations, one should keep in mind the claims of both relief and reform organizations. It is important to join the volunteer staff of a servicemen's center or to provide assistance for the poor. It is also important to prevent war or poverty. If a man saw numerous victims drowning in a river, he would be likely to jump in, pull them out one by one, and frantically administer artificial respiration. If then he should fall back, exhausted, and see the villain of the tale on a bridge upstream throw-

ing people into the river as fast as possible, he might conclude that it would be a better use of time and effort to
stand on the bridge and prevent men from being thrown
into the water in the first place.

Volunteers are needed, of course, both downstream and
upstream. Yet if one is forced to a choice, change in the
institutional structure to remove fundamental causes is
more important in the long run than is treating their
effects. Washing specks of minor corruption off our political hands or rinsing surface stain from our economic face
will not suffice. We must strike deeper toward the heart
of the matter. There are evils more profound than charity
can touch. We must also achieve a more fundamental justice in the basic structures of society.

Considering the full variety of problems confronting us,
there is no avoiding some choice of the most strategic spot
for service. If a person tries to do all the good, he is likely
to do no good. He becomes like butter in a cheap café,
spread so thin that it amounts to little at any one spot.
Instead of the words of Paul, "One thing I do" (Phil.
3:13), most of us, if we were honest, would have to
admit, "These forty-eleven things I dabble in."

Church people are very good at doing something just
to be doing something. Maximum creativity requires establishing priorities. Choose your cause. Concentrate your
resources. Deepen the impression made by sharpening the
point of your thrust. Even Jesus was not crucified on all
the crosses. The average person needs to devote himself
to one or two—or if he has a great deal of leisure, perhaps
three—areas of major interest. This does not mean that he
will not maintain an interest in other matters, or that he
will not support other persons specializing in additional
fields, in minor ways like financial contributions or incidental service. He will, however, accept the principle of
division of labor, a limitation on the areas in which any
single person continuously invests physical and intellectual "muscle" in the committee meetings, phone calls,

or steady correspondence that are necessary for effective action.

Emily Balch, well known for her contribution to the peace movement, once said: "When I was very young, I found myself tempted to join a movement for dress reform. But I resisted the temptation; people, I decided, who worked for one unpopular cause should be economical in practicing their 'queernesses.'" Susan B. Anthony likewise insisted, "I know only woman and her disfranchised." When asked to participate in the activities of another organization, she replied, "I can give neither time nor money to associations of women for any other purpose, however good it may be."

How, then, is a person to select the area for his attack? This decision is akin to a vocational choice. For the Christian it is a matter of discovering the area in which he is called by God to serve. Again, the key question to ask is this: At what point can a person of my capacities make the greatest contribution to human need? In assessing social need, one should look for the most basic, the most urgent, and the most neglected. Other things being equal, it is more important to work at the roots than at the fruits. By dealing with basic causes, one also contributes to improved outcomes. Major immediate threats must be dealt with to buy time for getting at other things. Norman Cousins, for example, recently recorded as his judgment, "The biggest lesson of all to be learned about contemporary civilization is that nothing anyone is doing today makes any sense unless it is connected to the making of a genuine peace." Also, where the line is most thinly manned, one's presence counts for most. The "pet charities" of the more casually concerned are likely to be fairly popular. The causes without rebels are often the most creative movements.

In whatever suitable area is selected for action, several guiding principles contribute to the most effective work. One of these is to learn before one acts, to listen before one speaks. This applies both within and outside the supporting group. Understanding human needs requires a listening that is more than understanding words. It is an attitude of life, a relationship of appreciation. As soon as an individual considers himself better than another, he is no longer carrying on a genuine dialogue. He is then tempted to begin doing all the talking himself and to imprison others in the chains of his goodwill. Many have tried vainly to help others without getting close to them. Openness to others is one way of loving. It is a way to learn what really needs to be done. It is also a way of establishing constructive relationships by conveying the status we assign to another person. In this respect we can speak with our ears. When we genuinely listen to another person we are saying to him: "You are important, a person worth learning from."

A second principle abundantly documented by the social sciences is that one wins future leadership within a group by supporting existing programs. Any member serves an apprenticeship before he is given a larger responsibility; he has no right to lead until he has learned to follow. Every man who wants to exert a creative influence within a group must also learn to conform to basic customs of the group. The right balance between creativity and conformity is not always easy to come by.

One way of expressing this sociological reality is in E. P. Hollander's concept of "idiosyncrasy credit." By this he means that each participant, by his conformity to group goals and his contribution to group projects, builds up a capital of acceptance. Such accumulated "idiosyncrasy credit" allows him to make innovations. If he uses up his capital too fast in forcing too great innovations, he undercuts his long-term effectiveness. No one should expect to be elected president of a group at the first meeting he attends. The pyramids of power are open, but promotion is preceded by hours of work in addressing envelopes, raising money, or other mundane projects of the group.

Nelson W. Polsby, in his *Community Power and Polit-ical Theory,* concludes, "There is a good deal of evidence that decision-makers become so by *self-selection*—pushing themselves into the leadership group by showing interest, willingness to work, and competence." They must have a certain amount of ability, but dedication also is important. Candidates for influence are scarce because many join and few become active. Leaders first prove their worth by work.

In this connection we need to learn not to despise mod-est areas. Someone needs to be a vice-president in charge of publicity or the chairman of the party brain trust. Others had better spend a great deal of time in the voting precincts. We need a higher view of the bottom, coupled with a willingness not only to start there but also to stay there. Anna Gordon, the secretary of Frances Willard, a leader in the temperance movement, often said that while she could not speak or write like her employer, she could mend her gloves and wash her stockings. By writing her letters, keeping accounts, and caring for her wardrobe, she allowed Frances Willard to move great crowds.

W. W. and L. J. Biddle use the phrase "microprocesses in the midst of macroprograms." Comprehensive programs on a grand scale are finally compounded of individual and local initiatives. Race riots are cooled by innumerable con-versations with gang leaders and city officials. The growth of every child involves the tying of many a shoestring. The ministry of Jesus frequently required placing one foot ahead of the other on walking tours with his disciples. At first glance, there may appear to be little romance in turn-ing a mimeograph handle or ringing doorbells, but this is the stuff of which social progress is made. Whether in local situations, subordinate positions, or inconspicuous action, modest areas are indispensable areas.

A fourth major guiding insight for the community par-ticipant has to do with developing creative interpersonal relationships. This is not the place for a full volume on the recommendations of psychologists on this subject. We do need to be reminded of the importance of understanding, acceptance, appreciation, and sensitivity to all those with whom we work. It is important to establish rapport and to recognize the deeper springs of action in persons rather than merely reacting superficially. Even though a person is deeply impatient with injustice, he must always be patient with persons, recognizing that significant growth is often slow and that others will act by their timetable instead of by ours. The reformer must often be willing to go halfway at the same time that he feels going all the way is long overdue. The quickest way in the long run may sometimes be the slow way in the short run. Inflammatory approaches are ordinarily to be avoided. One ought not become so emotionally involved as to distort the issues or exaggerate the charges. One city councilman, for example, in speaking to a group of laymen on the subject of political influence, pointed out that citizens petitioning the council ought never imply that councilmen are stupid scoundrels. On the contrary, they should assume that public officials in general are honest people trying to do a good job.

This is consistent with strong positive assertions in favor of a position. Resistance rooted in self-interest is not overcome by mild, innocuous approaches. There are extremes beyond which we cannot go without awakening negative reactions. At the same time research suggests that greater attitude change is stimulated when one takes a position which is considerably different from the person he is trying to persuade. In other words the creative person stands far enough ahead to demand attention, but not so far as to cut off contact entirely with most people.

Related to this is a fifth principle which asserts the superiority of democratic leadership. Better than either autocratic leadership (which dominates and manipulates followers) or a radically permissive approach (in which the "leader" does not exert himself) is a democratic pattern in which all members of the group actively share in discus-

sion and decision. The high-powered executive who dominates by pressure or prestige invites occasional rebellion
and never gains the benefit of full participation and support. Much better is a climate which encourages a genuine
pooling of insight. Each participant can become a percep-
tive enabler of the group process, balancing both an eagerness to learn from others with his own initiative in contributing to the group. One way of gaining the support of
strategic people is to involve them in the planning of a
project from the outset. In any community the unaffiliated
may become the disruptive.

Those who work in groups must pay attention to skills
in communication. They need to cultivate flexibility and
adaptability as new situations arise, not becoming so personally fixated on any one specific solution that they can
no longer admit they were wrong. These attitudes are not
inconsistent with vigorous presentation and energetic administration, but they do reflect a democratic social philosophy and a Christian regard for others which profoundly alters all presentation and administration.

Another general suggestion to be made is that those
active in community affairs become realistic about strategy. All social action is infected with ambiguity. Given
man as he is, rational arguments and calm persuasion may
not be enough to secure community improvement. Especially when resistance grows out of selfish interest and
entrenched power, coercion may also be necessary to en-
force justice. Just as society still needs laws and police, so
social reformers also need economic and social power.
Pressure groups may first try to persuade, but they may
then also have to withhold votes or economic patronage.
This does not mean acceptance of grossly immoral means
or violent methods, but it does mean realistic use of less
destructive power elements.

An effective community leader needs to develop a personal power base. If his words are to carry the greatest
weight, he must be backed by a group that votes and acts

with him. Such a need for a supporting group is an inevitable concomitant to democratic freedom in mass society.
A general policy emerges as a result of the confluence of
influence of subordinate groups. An individual carries
more weight in the councils of larger bodies if he is known
to have the confidence of significant subgroups. He must
sink his roots in a local group by which he is accepted and
for which he speaks. The labor federation official is
strengthened by the backing of a local union, the county
committeeman by a ward organization, and the churchman by a local congregation. One of the weaknesses of
the visionary or idealist may be such a preoccupation with
larger issues or theoretical solutions that he loses touch
with the people who need to support his solutions.

Any campaign for community improvement should be
aware of existing power structures. Wherever possible the
most influential people should be approached and the
major relevant subgroups involved. Any reforming group
needs to be equally aware of its supporters and of strate-
gically placed individuals or groups opposing them. For
example, in civil rights matters there are pivotal gatekeepers who may choose to keep the gates of opportunity
shut. These must be persuaded, pressured or replaced.
No amount of wishing will make it otherwise.

Realistic strategy begins with felt needs and existing
discontent, knowing that action starts and God is present
where people hurt. A campaign for such objectives needs
in turn to be divided into a series of limited objectives,
each possible to attain and therefore capable of providing
early experiences of success. One needs to begin where
people are in still another sense. To carry maximum conviction, any presentation must remember community sym-
bols, rituals and biases, all the way from the local baseball
team to the American way of life. A Yankee in Santo
Domingo should learn to give the *abrazo* readily. A peace
worker in a fashionable suburb handicaps his cause by
dirty fingernails or wearing a full beard.

Publicity and public relations are important in a culture that provides many bids for attention. As William Muehl puts it: "God sees what is secret and rewards in secret. Politicians do not have this divine quality about them." The beat of a band may have little to do with the slogans on the banners, but it does attract people to the parade. At the same time, of course, it is necessary to recognize deeper social pressures that must be dealt with in ways more profound than surface publicity.

Those taking ministry to the community seriously have available to them all the usual strategies involved in education, negotiation, economic pressure, and political action. Their education for service should include an introduction to the major possibilities in each of these four areas. Whenever necessary, less conventional aspects of these approaches may be called for. Resolutions may have to be backed by demonstrations when resistance is great. On some issues tensions and divisions have to be increased before change is possible. The sociologist helps us to recognize that conflict may be a necessary prelude to progress and deeper harmony. Our problem is to manage conflict as well as possible and to work at a final reconciliation that is as thorough as possible.

As a sufficiently diversified strategy is necessary, so a comprehensive enough program is essential. One goal often depends on the achievement of another. Full opportunity for minority races depends on economic measures to deal with poverty. Or, there are limits to our international influence so long as we do not maintain law and order on our streets at home.

In addition to a primary investment of energy in a particular problem, each of us can give incidental support to a longer list of organizations and programs. For the most creative impact we need both to spread support and to concentrate involvement. A few pages back it was suggested that no man should spread himself too thin and that each participant in a particular movement should ration his eccentricities. This is a principle of concentrated focus of energy. It does not, however, contradict whatever spread of support we can accomplish in ways that do not significantly handicap our high priority commitment.

There are forms of support that do not take sizable amounts of time and energy, and that are not so eccentric as to lead to a negative reaction. These kinds of contribution a man can make to race relations or the treatment of juvenile delinquency even though the more absorbing concern of his life is world peace. A man can add his name to the membership list of a number of creative organizations even though he is not active in all of them. He can take a moment to sign a petition circulated by a friend who is specializing in another area of change just as our friends can in turn sign our petitions, thus strengthening all the movements concerned.

An important way to support both primary and secondary concerns is through financial contributions. To our previous injunctions to creativity expressed in the words "talk" and "join" may be added the word "give." Where our hearts are, there should our treasure be also. Wherever God is at work in the world, there he would have his material resources directed by his stewards. Empty treasuries and worthy causes are often associated. Additional dollars, like persons, count for more where there are fewer of them already at work. The regular writing of well-directed checks, even though they seem small, is still significant. Perhaps the checks would not remain so small if we remembered that we are the affluent of the earth and that more is required from those who are more fortunate. Whatever ought to be said about a redistribution of wealth between persons or countries, a great deal must be said about redistributing our own wealth between less urgent private wants and the most crucial social needs.

A related general avenue to social influence is spending one's money discriminately. If God and mammon are to be properly related, our money ought to express our convictions rather than having our convictions grow out of our wealth. One aspect of monetary witness is to buy with a conscience, creating social influence through purchasing power. Patronage increases the seller's profits and makes it more likely that he will succeed. It is a way of casting a vote in favor of the policies of the supplier. In this way consumers have a certain amount of control in our economy. This is a positive version of the boycott. It involves the use of selective patronage to support policies we consider desirable. Selection is inevitable. We cannot buy everything that is offered. There is no compelling reason for buying a television set from every dealer in town and of every brand that each dealer offers. The question is, Do we make our selections on the basis of impulse, advertising, personal savings, or social concern? Letting our ethical standards influence our buying is simply an expression of integrity. We cannot in good conscience make immorality profitable. We must in good conscience make socially responsible business enterprises more likely to succeed.

In a very real sense, the patron of a sweatshop wears on his back the blood of the seamstresses exploited there. On the other hand, the families that patronize only higher-quality movies to a certain extent affect even Hollywood. As a part of education for peace, some have refused to buy war toys. One group of parents used the slogan, "Let's disarm the nursery." It would be socially wholesome if larger groups of consumers reacted negatively to misleading advertising, refusing to buy such brands which used objectionable publicity campaigns.

The sensitivity of John Woolman ought to stir modern consciences at this point. Being convinced that dyes were being used that harmed workers, he wore undyed garments. He refused to use sugar that had been produced by slave labor. Even on his deathbed he consented to use only medicines that "did not come through defiled channels or oppressive hands." Often for us only a rough approximation is possible because we lack full information about the policies of purveyors of goods and services. Depending on our social philosophy, we may even differ about the sources of the guidance we consider most helpful or reliable. Some will make use of the union label, motion-picture ratings by educational groups, or occasional information from consumers' research agencies. In any case, buying with greater sensitivity of conscience requires a recognition that the general scramble by consumers to get the most for the least may be highly antisocial, and that there are larger issues of justice involved than we have commonly realized.

With respect to all the matters discussed in this chapter, each of us needs to meditate on his Christian citizenship quotient. Without suggesting that it can be calculated with computerized exactitude, we can reflect on how well we have accepted our responsibility for the community by using some very rough indicators. The stubs in our checkbooks indicate the range of our concern—whether it stops with the family, or adds the church and conventional charities, or goes beyond these to more neglected needs. The activities that take place in our living rooms indicate whether we are family-bound, or limited to entertaining friends, or hosting conversations and committees on the community level. Do the uses to which our telephones are put include the adult equivalent of lengthy teen-age chatter, or directions to tradesmen to keep the material aspects of the household running smoothly, or some solicitation of funds and memberships for world-changing organizations? The entries on our individual appointment calendars are a sensitive indicator. Are they predominantly recreational, educational, or expressions of creative citizenship? Intelligence quotients and personality quotients are undoubtedly important, but if intelligent, well-adjusted personalities are to continue to live on this planet, or if intelligence and mental health are to have a supporting social environment, we shall also need to develop high citizenship quotients.

5

Politics for Amateurs

THE CIVIL RIGHTS ACT of 1964 may well go down in history as the key piece of legislation in this revolutionary struggle for equal opportunity for all citizens. Hubert H. Humphrey, the Senate floor manager for the bill, was convinced that the churches were "the most important force at work" on behalf of the measure. A Kansas congressman put it more colloquially and antagonistically when he said: "I'd like to vote against it, but I can't. The church groups are on my tail." Large numbers of churchmen were active across the country and in Washington. A feature of the campaign was a daily worship service in a nearby church on Capitol Hill. This intimate relationship between worship and political action has repeatedly characterized the Christian faith.

Christianity has generally had a positive attitude toward the state. The statement in Rom., ch. 13, that the governing authorities "have been instituted by God" is not acceptably interpreted to mean that any regime in power, regardless of how corrupt it may be, has the blessing of God. But the passage does suggest that a social institution of political authority is in accordance with God's purposes. A human environment of order and justice is a goal for all men. The state is necessary to secure these, and Christians therefore are to regard the state as an important means toward higher ends. Churchmen can work through the state for Christian purposes. Any adequate theology of politics would insist that unless we use effective means toward righteous ends, our religion becomes irrelevant to the entire social process.

Christians must always be deeply concerned about historical processes, because they see God working in history for the realization of his intentions. If we take history seriously, then we must also take politics seriously, for decisions made through the state are a major factor in the outcome of historical struggle. When we stand aside from political events, we illustrate the words of C. Wright Mills, "History is made behind men's backs."

Increasingly, if one is to be where the action is, he must act politically. Whether we like it or not, more and more social decisions are made through political structures. How many juvenile delinquents will there be in my neighborhood next year? Will there be enough jobs to go around? Will the world experience peace or war? All these questions will be to a great extent answered by the action of political units. Every citizen has justifiable expectations including, for example, police protection against being raped or robbed, enough pure water when he turns on his faucet, good schools for his children, well-maintained roads, protection against depressions and foreign invasion. In the modern world these expectations can be realized only through political action. Not only then should the citizen be prepared to pay taxes for such services, but he should also expect to give some sort of tithe of time to politics, a rightful share of energy which is his appropriate quota. Decisions affecting millions of people are now being made through political channels. The question, Should the church or churchmen be in politics? then needs to be rephrased to ask, Should the church influence such major social outcomes? If we seriously intend to serve man, we cannot avoid political expression. This was illustrated in a cartoon that portrayed a portly congressman meeting a clergyman coming up the Capitol steps. The legislator asked: "What are you doing here? I thought

you were supposed to be taking care of the flock?" The
minister replied: "I am. I am after the wolf." Washington, the state capital, and United Nations headquarters
can now appropriately be considered mission fields.

When we say "God was in Christ reconciling the world
to himself" (II Cor. 5:19), theology immediately gets all
mixed up in politics. In this central proclamation of the
Christian faith the life of God and the life of man in
the world are joined. We stand before God as we stand in
the world. We find our vocation here. If God works in us,
the witness of our lives is a witness in the world of men,
at every point that seriously counts. When we speak of
God's activity in the world we are forced to include words
about peace and justice and freedom. This is part of what
Harvey Cox means when he says, "Speaking of God must
be political." Because the historical church has been
rather consistently clear about this, it has a long record
of witness directed toward political leaders. As a prece-
dent, the leading figures of the Old Testament were
deeply involved in politics. The prophets spoke to kings
about both domestic policy and international alliances.
While the range of witness of the early church was not as
wide as it might have been, Rome was quite correct in
seeing the growing church as a threat to some of the practices of the Empire. Throughout intervening centuries a
large part of church history had to do with recommendations and controversies with secular rulers. When someone today asks, Should the church go into politics?, he
is really misstating the question. He should be asking,
Should the church get out of politics?

In both service and witness, politics is a way of expressing love to neighbor in practical ways. To beat swords
into plowshares or to do justice to the poor means getting
into politics. If we are even to interpret the meaning of
love to modern man, we must increasingly do so in concrete social terms many of which are political in nature.
Acting politically is now one important way of saying to

modern man what the Christian message is. As Philippe Maury has put it, political action is "the language of evangelism." Since both Christian proclamation and action are involved, a nonpolitical pattern of existence is rejection of our stewardship of life's resources, a way of nullifying the call of God.

Two important arguments on the other side deserve consideration. It is often felt that the Christian should have nothing to do with politics because it is a dirty business. A politician is sometimes defined as one who manages public affairs for private advantage. Too common is the popular saying, "In politics a man must learn to rise above principle." In the first place, these statements constitute a libel on politicians. Every human organization is continuously infected by man's propensity toward evil. Certainly some scoundrels have found a hideout in politics. It is doubtful, however, whether the percentage is any higher than in other social institutions, and the unscrupulous cynic again and again is balanced by the highly motivated idealist who also finds his way into political circles. In the second place, even if the charge against politicians were true, the Christian would have to reply that just because the business is dirty is all the more reason for participation in order to make a redemptive contribution. "Those who are well have no need of a physician, but those who are sick." (Matt. 9:12.) The more corrupt a situation is, the louder is its summons to Christian action.

Particularly is this true since an invasion of Christian influence can alter the character of politics. The number active in the inner circle of political groups is usually small. Few people attend political clubs, canvass the precincts, or vote at party conventions. The number who are grossly self-seeking or immoral is even smaller. A comparatively small cadre of Christians can therefore have decisive influence. Often quoted from Mark Twain is the statement: "Reader, suppose you were an idiot, and suppose you were a member of Congress. But I repeat myself." If this insinuation is ever true, it is because the population in general has acted idiotically. Jerry Voorhis, out of a considerable background of experience in Congress, was convinced that "as few as a dozen capable, intelligent, and determined people can in the course of four to six years change the representation in any congressional district in America."

A second objection to Christian participation in political action is that politics is of necessity the art of compromise and that the Christian should never lower standards in this way. It is true that in order to gather majority support, political proposals must strike a least common denominator appealing to the interests of a variety of groups. It is ordinarily necessary to gain support from those who are not yet ready to go the whole way. Successful action is always a matter of next steps or half a loaf. This led Lord Morley to say, "Politics is a field where action is one long second-best, and where the choice constantly lies between two blunders."

This, however, constitutes no valid objection to Christian participation. As has been previously pointed out, the person who proposes to act creatively in the existing world must always act realistically in terms of what is actually possible. This is the only way to make a contribution. It is by short stumbling steps that we move in an imperfect world. This is usually all the progress there is. During the height of the League of Nations debate in 1919, one newspaper said, "God made the world in seven days, but he didn't have a Senate to deal with." Yet it is with senates or schools or churches that God works. In many areas other than politics, when we join God we heed his summons to action that is the best possible under the circumstances. Whenever a man eats a sandwich, he is implicated in an economic process that also involves compromise. Even when he joins the church he has accepted organizational practices that often differ considerably from the Sermon on the Mount. Not to eat or join the church or act politically is an even more serious compromise. The attempt to withdraw from sinful humanity behind sheltering monastic walls is itself greater sin. The highest ethical impulse is not to leave the world to its worst elements, but rather to immerse oneself in the common life exerting an unremitting tug to keep the tension tight between the ultimate goal and immediate possibilities.

After all, politics describes the way in which population-wide decisions are made in a democracy. Either we master the strategy of politics or we lose the values of democracy as a way of life. No one of us would join a demonstration and shout, "Death to Democracy"—but we do worse. We devote our lives to the realization of that slogan by our political inaction. As Edmund Burke put it, "The only thing necessary for the triumph of evil is for good men to do nothing." Several phrases commonly used to rationalize inaction actually are signals of the decline of democratic vitality. These include, "This really is not an important enough issue on which to take a stand." "I don't know enough about the subject to speak." "What can one man do?" "People are divided on this." "After all, I have to make a living." There are issues big enough to deserve study on which one man can make enough difference to deserve sacrifice. Part of the price of freedom is breaking down the major form of segregation reflected in the view that religion and politics do not mix.

The case for Christian participation in politics becomes even clearer when we make an important distinction between action by individual Christians and official action by the church. It is the first that we are most particularly talking about in this chapter. That individuals motivated by their faith should be politically active would be widely accepted even by those who object to somewhat similar action by the church.

There is one important, though limited, restriction that ought to be placed on official actions of the church. This grows out of the fact that the church as an organization does have a unique function not shared to the same extent by any other social institution. The church ought continuously to bear witness to a standard of perfection, the will of God, before which every act of man is brought under judgment. While the Christian norm is always relevant as goal, it is also always transcendent over every particular human decision. To protect its distinctive witness, the church cannot become identified with highly ambiguous or seriously compromised action. When it does this, its actions speak so loudly as to drown out its words. "Let the church be the church" is a slogan often used to express this point.

On the other hand, in order to convey any challenging social meaning at all, the church must speak somewhat specifically, even though in this world speaking specifically means introducing some ambiguity. Too great generalizations can too easily be selectively interpreted to fit whatever is our prevailing prejudice. The church remains innocuous and ineffectual if it talks only about love, freedom, justice, and the glories of motherhood. Persons of all political persuasions, in sharp conflict on many of the issues of the day, would equally claim to be acting in full accord with these ideals. Therefore, the problem of the church in its official action as an organization is always to take a position that involves minimal ambiguity and to draw a line at the most serious compromises, in order to keep the moral claim as demanding as possible on both its individual members and the general public. This is one major reason for the church's very existence.

This means, for example, that the church should probably never endorse modern war. No matter what justification may exist for a particular conflict, the evils involved in war are so great that the church must keep maximum pressure on all of us to find better methods in international relations. Individual Christians may participate in war or become conscientious objectors according to the dictates of their consciences. The church may encourage them to make such a decision at the same time that in its official statements and actions it preserves its unique institutional purpose. The vocation of individual churchmen is at such points different from the vocation of the church as an organization. (Other organized bodies, like business corporations or service clubs, also make this distinction, allowing freedom to members to do many things on which the organization as such takes no position.)

The same line of reasoning would suggest that the church as an organization ordinarily should not endorse political candidates or parties. Issues are always seriously mixed in the positions of candidates or the platforms of parties. While they may be reasonably right on some issues, they are likely to be considerably wrong on others, or their positions on issues may be beyond criticism while personal motivation and character may be questionable. If the church endorses such a miscellaneous scrambling of right and wrong, it is no longer making a clear witness. The Amsterdam Assembly of the World Council of Churches was right in advising, "The church as such should not be identified with any political party, and it must not act as though it were itself a political party." If ever the angel Gabriel were running on the Kingdom of God ticket, then this limitation would no longer apply. That is scarcely foreseeable under present circumstances! However, it is more likely that on occasion a rather thoroughly satanic Hitler-like candidate may be running on such a morally reactionary platform that the church might properly oppose him by name. At the same time, however, the church might stop short of officially endorsing the other candidate.

Again God's calling to the individual church member is different, since his role in society is different. In his personal capacity a churchman must make choices even when the issues are highly mixed. In the light of the goals emphasized by the church he should endorse parties and candidates. Inspired by his church, he keeps the tension tight between practical possibility and ultimate goal. This he does at his working post of day-to-day practical detail where extremely ambiguous choices cannot be avoided. His political activity roots in worship, and he makes his specific choices in the light of the whole meaning of reality. This is his unique contribution to the quality of civic affairs.

The one limitation attached to the political witness of the church is not to be suggested on grounds that political analysis is difficult. Church leaders must pay the price of whatever preparation is required to achieve the necessary competence in understanding complex matters. This does not require them to become specialists on the level of administrative details, but like other leaders of popular opinion they need to acquire adequate understanding on the level of general policy on major matters. This they can do, and this the church must do. Nor is this limitation on partisan endorsement of candidates and parties suggested in order to avoid division in the church and withdrawal of pledges by disgruntled members. On important matters it is not nearly so important that the church keep all her members as that she remain faithful to her Lord. Often the church, after full discussion and with reasonable consensus, must speak on highly controversial and crucial matters. On the other hand, restraint by the church in regard to candidates and parties is suggested in order that the church may speak the more clearly and the more powerfully, raising a standard that is less likely to be misunderstood and is more likely to keep maximum pressure on society for speedy improvement.

The same principal is further illustrated in the kinds of positions the church should take on specific issues. As has been pointed out, to speak meaningfully it must speak with a degree of specificity on major subjects before the public, including bills before the legislature, referendum propositions on the ballot, or items in party platforms. Here too, some concrete proposals may be a highly mixed bag of ingredients. For example, if the church should happen to believe in both public housing and unsegregated housing, and a particular bill before the Congress should make possible segregated public housing, the church could scarcely fulfill its function by endorsing the bill. If the parliamentary situation allowed for no amendment, individual churchmen in Congress would have to weigh the values and vote on the measure. To speak with greatest clarity and most impelling meaning, however, the church as an organization normally had better take a position, not on the bill, but on the component issues, continuing to ask for both public housing and unsegregated housing. In other cases, of course, where there is no significant ambiguity the church should not hesitate to endorse a particular bill.

In the light of this discussion, what then is the proper role of the minister of a church? On the one hand, he is an individual citizen bound to accept the full obligations of participation, including endorsement of parties and candidates. On the other hand, he is also frequently the official representative of the church. In the latter case, as when he is sent to testify before a legislative committee, he is bound by the limits set for action by the church as an institution. On other occasions, when he converses in the barbershop or marks a ballot in the voting booth, he acts as an individual citizen. He then has the same rights and obligations as do other citizens. His congregation ought to accept that fact and give him that freedom. After all, we do this in other situations. When the minister disciplines his children, or has sex relations with his wife, or chooses a brand of cereal for his breakfast table, everyone knows that he is not acting in his official capacity as a representative of the church. Why should not ministers, provided that they clearly state that they are acting in their individual capacities, not have the privilege of taking a position on controversial issues or even participating in political campaigns?

It has been argued that it is impossible to avoid the
popular assumption that a minister is implicating the
church in his actions. The consequences of such an objection are unexpectedly far reaching and dramatically
devastating. If it is impossible for a minister to separate
individual from institutional action, then no one else can
either. To follow this logic, corporation executives would
have to withdraw from all political participation lest they
implicate their firms, and every member of a service club
would have to lapse into complete silence lest the Rotar-
ians or the Kiwanians be enmeshed in his actions. The
only persons then who could engage in political activity
would be the self-employed and the unaffiliated. This
conceivably might include gamblers, bootblacks, and a
few other similar groups. Actually, of course, we avoid
such wholesale disenfranchisement by constantly distinguishing between the individual and the institutional role
he plays. The clergy should not suffer cruel and unusual
discrimination in this respect. Presumably, they bring
some educational preparation, ethical insight, or spiritual
motivation which should be made available in steering
the ship of state. To exclude any professional group is to
impoverish the democratic process.

Some have argued that if they knew that the minister
on Saturday night had addressed a partisan political rally
(especially of the opposition party), they would find it
difficult to receive Communion from his hand on Sunday
morning. Careful reflection suggests that this also is a
decidedly immature opinion. For one thing, if a person
is fully aware of the nature of the democratic process, he
does not feel antagonistic when someone sincerely takes a
position different from his own. Rather, he expects that
many will do so. He continues group discussion with
them, and this constitutes no barrier to personal relationships. He knows that the group process in the "miracle of
dialogue" produces the most creative synthesis only when
all participants freely and fully express their positions. It

is important that every man assume the responsibilities of citizenship. We really ought to conclude that unless the minister consistently did something like speaking to a political group on Saturday night, we would find it harder to receive Communion from his hands, because we would know that he was shirking an important way of serving his neighbor. Observing the clergyman as a consumer eating eggs produced through an economy that is something less than fully Christian should not cause us to discredit his sermons. Why should we then be horrified if the minister-citizen makes a political campaign speech?

A letter once written by Henry Ward Beecher deserves more widespread appreciation today. He said: "Allow me first to thank you for that sound sense which leads you to judge that, in such a time as this, a clergyman should be interested and active in the affairs of the public. . . . In a democratic community, it is not safe for any body of men to live above or outside of the circle of common citizenship. . . . When men speak of political duty as degrading to a minister, they dishonor and degrade our institutions and our primary ideas of citizenship. It ought to be an honor to serve the State in the ranks. It ought to be taught in the family, in the school, and in the pulpit, that it is a fault, a sin, for any man to be unconcerned in political duties. . . . When the framing of laws, the elections of magistrates, the discussion of public civil interests, and the sacred function of the Vote, are regarded as degrading to a religious man, the Republic is already on the broad road to destruction! We must exalt citizenship. We must make its duties sacred. We must excuse no man from the full performance."

Along with rights to claim, the minister has responsibilities to respect. He ought carefully to make it clear that any personal party expression is made as an individual and not in his official capacity. If he uses his church letterhead in writing his congressman, for example, he should include somewhere in the letter a sentence to disassociate

his church from his stand, thus providing the letterhead
only as a return address and as a general occupational
identification. If he signs a statement, he should require
that any publication of names be accompanied by the no-
tation that organizational affiliations are listed for identification only. Furthermore, a minister must lean over
backwards to make sure that his pastoral ministry does not
discriminate against parishioners who disagree with him.
As with any hobby or other avocational pursuit, he must
keep his political activities within bounds and properly
subordinated to the total claim of his ministry. In all that
he does, he ought to avoid dogmatism and maintain a high
level of content and attitude. It is by such a careful and
considerate approach that he confirms the freedom that is
rightly his.

An even more serious matter is that both ministers and
laity are neophytes at the game of politics. Our tricycle
thrusts are therefore buried under the bulldozer power of
selfish interest groups. It has been suggested that our
society leaves two of the most difficult and important jobs
in the world to amateurs, namely, parenthood and citizenship. At least we can try increasingly to educate the
amateurs beyond the kind of seemingly obvious, but actually dangerous, aphorisms that are widely accepted. A
favorite story among politicians concerns the senator who
was asked to what principles he attributed his political
success. "To three rules of conduct from which I have
never deviated," he replied. "First, be bold as a lion on a
rising tide. Second, when the water reaches the upper
deck, follow the rats. Third, and most important of all,
when in doubt, do right!" In current political action by
churchmen one can list comparable fallacies, half-truths
which often become total error. In particular, four fatal
flaws may be mentioned which can be turned into four
certain strengths.

For one thing, idealists easily oversimplify the issues,
relying on a kind of moralism which sees only part of the

total picture. A national Protestant magazine once desig-
nated a South Carolina senator as its statesman of the year
because he did not drink or allow alcohol to be served in
his home. Not asked were questions about his attitudes on
race or international affairs which have often contradicted
the position of the denomination publishing the magazine. There were churchmen in Germany in Nazi days
who supported Hitler, arguing that he must be a good man
because he did not drink or smoke. This kind of confusion
about major and minor issues can lead to all sorts of
bizarre endorsements. Another illustration of oversimplification is the stock argument that can be advanced against
almost any new law, namely, that it will limit liberty. This
consequence obviously follows for minorities who wish to
disobey the proposed legislation, but the argument over-
looks the fact that in a government of laws, wise legislation
also protects the liberty of majorities. The argument as it
is often used is beside the point and neglects the major
issues that ought to be faced.

The simplicity of innocence which precedes serious
consideration is a danger to political action. It can be
transformed into strength if we push on to the simplicity beyond complexity. There is a kind of maturity that
comes from facing ambiguity and discovering a pattern
of creativity through compromise. Instead of our avoiding complexity or being overwhelmed by it, a model can
emerge that gives us reliable guidance. For example, one
of the most frustrating situations faced by the churchman
is a choice between two candidates—a comparative scoun-
drel who agrees with the churchman on important issues
and a near saint who does not agree. A too simple moralism has frequently led Christians under these circumstances to support candidates because of their personal
qualities instead of their social philosophy. A more mature
analysis might lead one to conclude that this may or may
not be sound depending on the kind of office for which the
candidate is running. If the election concerns law enforce-

ment, then personal integrity may indeed be the more important of the two considerations. If on the other hand, the office at stake is concerned with legislation or policy determination, then the social philosophy of the candidate is more important. It makes little difference what candidates for dogcatcher think about a Middle East crisis, but in voting for a senator it is important to know his views about foreign policy. One, of course, would prefer to have a saint who is also sound. If one has to choose between lesser mortals, it is better to have a senator who supports policies contributing to international justice even though he puts his nephew on his office payroll than to have a lawmaker who avoids nepotism but makes war more likely. A too simple moralism would lead to rejecting the man who might support what the voter wants, in favor of the man who, because of his personal integrity, is sure to do what the voter does not want.

A second common failing is preoccupation with generalities that carry no message to Washington or any other place at which decisions are made. Contentment with generalization is often the outgrowth of a naïve utopianism that assumes that men will immediately see the relevance of a high ideal, and will act to implement it with obvious social structures. This mistake was illustrated by a campaign conducted by one major denomination for letters to congressmen urging them to support world order. One congressman, in exasperation, said to a leader of the denomination: "Why don't you call these churchmen off? They are flooding my desk with mail but I do not know what they want." A general concept such as world order has to be translated into the number of a specific congressional bill, or at least into the kind of specific proposals that could be found in such a bill.

The difficulty is illustrated by the story of a young minister in a new parish. During his first week he was horrified that his parishioners in this lumbering community were pulling logs out of the river that had been cut by lumbermen upstream. They cut off the identifying mark on the end and replaced it with their own mark so that they would receive credit for it when it floated down to the mill. On the following Sunday he preached an impassioned sermon on the text, "Thou shalt not steal." After enthusiastically congratulating their new minister, they proceeded the next week to carry on exactly the same practices. On the following Sunday the minister preached his sermon on the text, "Thou shalt not saw off the end of thy neighbor's log."

Supporting a reform in only general terms may in effect make it less likely to succeed. Such attempts do not win support for the specific measures that are necessary, and they may even confirm opponents in their existing position. Misdirected support is the equivalent of doing nothing and plays into the hands of the dominant power. This was the weakness of the white liberal who at the same time that he made general statements about racial injustice was apathetic about the actions necessary to change concrete situations. He actually accepted the continuation of the *status quo* because he was not willing to do what was necessary to change it. His goodwill was thoroughly discredited because he refused to combine reliable goals with specific strategies, the key to political strength.

A third fatal flaw is the expectation of too easy success. When white knights come riding, churchmen often expect righteousness immediately to win, in something comparable to the thirty minutes it takes the "good guys" on television. This anticipation of sudden results permits easy discouragement when strong opposition appears. We forget that it is possible to lose many times and yet win the final battle. Our enthusiasm becomes spasmodic or short-lived in a kind of "hit and run" politics. When we have won a point in a civic clean-up campaign, we may retire from the struggle only to find that the tainted crew we turned out soon comes back again. Good people often get tired of being good before bad people get tired of being bad.

Or, we may settle for too shallow an involvement, expecting too great results from too little effort. We may occasionally write our congressman, forgetting that this is only the kindergarten stage of political action. We may talk about what should be done but never carry through. We may think that speaking a reasonable word should be sufficient when the resistance of deeply entrenched interests requires pressure, conflict, and suffering. We may be willing to lend our name for use on a letterhead but never offer a further hand. Words originally spoken to Wayne B. Wheeler by Mark Hanna still apply to contemporary churchmen. "Young man," said he, "your kind of people are all right in a prayer meeting, but they are no good at a caucus."

Again, this fatal idea can be transformed into a certain strength. The trick is to preserve the enthusiasm of the fresh recruit, storming into party headquarters for the first time. We can do with a good deal less jaded cynicism on the part of entrenched old-timers. At the same time, enthusiasm must be tied to a realistic enlistment for the full rigors of the campaign. The right combination is to yoke Pegasus to a plow. As the citizen-soldier expects his life to be cruelly unpleasant, so may the citizen-politician. This is no news to the Christian. Knowing the world for what it is, he expects aspects of life to be hard.

Before his Supreme Court days, while he was vigorously immersed in pioneering civil rights through the National Association for the Advancement of Colored People, Thurgood Marshall once said, "Isn't it nice that no one cares which twenty-three hours of the day I work?" Turgot, when accused of impatience reacted with a similar spirit: "I cannot help it! The needs of the people are immense, and in my family gout carries us off at fifty."

So long as they introduce into life the balance between relaxation and activity that is necessary for the greatest effectiveness, Christians recognize this kind of claim. They know the persistence Jesus was talking about when he spoke of putting one's hand to the plow (Luke 9:62). Catherine of Siena rebuked one of her followers who had given up a mission to France after having been cowed by the arrest of a companion: "If you could not walk there, you could have crawled; if you could not go as a friar, you could have gone as a pilgrim; if you had no money, you could have begged your way there." William Lloyd Garrison was so stirred up over slavery that he wrote in the first issue of *The Liberator:* "I will be as harsh as truth and as uncompromising as justice. On this subject I do not wish to think, or speak, or write, with moderation. . . . I am in earnest. I will not equivocate—I will not excuse— I will not retreat a single inch—and I will be heard."

A fourth enfeebling fallacy in political action concerns the myth of the independent voter. One form that this takes is an undue intensification of individualism in politics. Many of us are enamored by the spirit of the lone hero of the television Western who spurs away to head off the desperadoes at Dry Gulch Pass. After the chase we are convinced that the bare knuckles of one righteous man can be the downfall of any ten or twenty others. Even though in other areas of our existence we have enlisted as organization men, in politics we often remain prejudiced against organization. This attitude reflects a failure also in our theology, since we temporarily overlook that full manhood is found through membership in community. The result is that our influence is fragmented and feeble. Men of virtue are not automatically elected to public office because of their virtue but because they have an organization behind them.

A second danger in the independent voter image is that it may exaggerate the morality of nonpartisanship. Churchmen are easily convinced that they should not be firmly committed to any one political party but should remain free to swing their support from one to the other.

There is half a truth here. Amateurs moving into politics often can contribute a healthy emphasis to issues rather than to party. Under some circumstances one can work more effectively for a particular objective independently of established parties. Everyone should avoid the blindness of partisanship, or the inability to see things objectively because he is a "true believer." Within a party structure there should be a degree of independence about the Christian since he is always leaning and tugging in the direction of something better than can possibly be adopted at any given time. In a very real sense, on the morning after each election won by his own party, he ought to go into "His Majesty's loyal opposition" within his party, working to improve the action of the newly elected leaders.

Yet, there is nothing particularly Christian about remaining uncommitted in such ways as are necessary to effect change. There are certain kinds of political influence that one can have only inside a party organization. Crucial conclusions have been reached long before an election occurs. Candidates have been selected and platforms adopted by the insiders. Ballots are cast not only on election day but in party caucuses, central committees, and conventions. The citizen who waits for the final ballot is presented with only two of the original alternatives. Albert T. Rasmussen sums this up by saying, "The individual voter who comes out of political hiding on election day to cast his secret ballot fails to enter the real process of the formation of policy."

For those Christians who feel called to full political participation, the greatest strength normally is found as they hang on even though they "hang loose." As is true of their relationship to the world, they are in the party but not of it, always recognizing a superior citizenship in the Kingdom of God. They are prophetic partisans, remaining in critical collaboration with those groups which are essential to the decision-making process.

In political life it is possible to be a mere spectator,

listening to returns as one would hear the report of a sports event, with dramatic uncertainty about what the final score will be. Or, one can be a minicitizen, simply casting one's vote, which is the irreducible level of participation. This may become even "more irreducible" if the ballot is a thoughtless vote for the party that one has "inherited" from his family, his region, or his social group. Relying on such minimal involvement is a fantasyland view of politics, a naïve approach to the processes of democracy. Yet, the majority of the population only infrequently goes beyond this. Lester W. Milbrath constructs a hierarchy of political involvement that ranges from such things as voting, attempting to convince another voter, wearing a button, or putting a sticker on his car, through contacting public officials or attending political rallies, to contributing time in a political campaign, soliciting funds, or actually holding public office. On the basis of available evidence, he concludes that from 40 to 70 percent of the population may vote in any given election, that 25 or 30 percent may try to proselyte others, that about 15 percent display a button or sticker, that about 13 percent contact public officials, 10 percent make monetary contributions, and only about 5 percent are active in a party or in campaigns. In his *Political Participation,* he summarizes: "About one-third of the adult American population can be characterized as politically apathetic or passive; in most cases, they are unaware, literally, of the political part of the world around them. Another 60 percent play largely spectator roles in the political process; they watch, they cheer, they vote, but they do not do battle." Some among us would not find life much different under a dictatorship, since even now we are not using the freedoms available to us.

It is true that we have many gifts and diverse callings. Some will properly invest their creative citizenship time in the plant or the office or the church, without engaging in a lengthy variety of political activities. Yet every Christian from time to time ought to do more than vote. This means keeping at hand a list of effective activities for the amateur. What are such major paths to political power for the common man? The discussion that follows excludes suggestions for laymen who hold political office. Theirs is an important function. Christians who hold office ought to have a great deal to say to one another. The wider need, however, is for suggestions for all citizens that are concrete enough to dispel some of the forbidding mystery of unfamiliar territory. Such suggestions can be made under four headings, including public-opinion formation, persuasion of officials, political club participation, and campaign activities.

The first of these, public-opinion formation, is important because politicians must in the long run pay attention to any important ground swell of popular conviction. The climate of citizen desire fixes limits and points directions for public policy. Direct contact with officials has less effect if it has little public backing. A former congressman, Byron L. Johnson, out of his own experience and observation, advised: "If you think letter writing is a substitute for education, agitation, and propagation of your faith, you are one hundred eighty degrees wrong. Do this first, then write your letters."

The cultivation of public opinion may involve all the educational devices that were suggested in the previous chapter in connection with community influence. Such "grass-roots lobbying" can be done through conversation, discussion groups, mass meetings, newspaper ads, organizational resolutions, or citizens committees on specific issues. One effective combination approach is to multiply study groups of thoughtful people, selected members of which will later join a speaker's bureau to talk to a variety of small or larger groups that can be interested. Any accurate representation of the power structure of a community will recognize a whole infrastructure of various kinds of organizations at the bottom through which individuals can have their say.

A person committed to a campaign may wish that he owned a newspaper or a television station. Yet, even without such fortunate forms of wealth he can often have access to mass media. Groups can create news through large conferences or unusual small occurrences. Press releases and pictures can then be supplied to the important media. If enough people contribute, they can buy advertising space, or a committee can approach media officials like editors or television executives to change their attitudes on either coverage or position on public issues. Anyone with a pen and an idea can write a "letter to the editor."

Large numbers of comparatively helpless people can call attention to their ideas through public demonstrations. Parades or mass meetings allow people to vote with their feet or to speak through the presence of their bodies. This is a time-honored mode of public expression used, for example, by women suffragists and war veterans. Such demonstrations deepen the commitment of those who participate, attract newspaper reporters and television cameras, and make a more dramatic public appeal. Since using such a method too often dulls its effect, it should probably be reserved for issues of prime importance. Some traditionalist observers may be antagonized by such tactics, but if responsibly done by respectable people, a silent vigil in front of the city hall or a march from the outskirts of a hypothetical circle of thermonuclear destruction to a downtown "ground zero" may constructively stimulate the general public.

Oftentimes, agitation for improvement has been left to those most aggrieved. At the moment there is considerable stress on mobilizing the poor and the racial minorities in our inner cities, yet the political decisions that affect poverty and civil rights will be made more in the suburbs than in the slums. The slums are where most of the voters live, and where most of the readers of this book can immediately work. No man is exempt from some active contribution to public-opinion formation.

A second general area for political action is communication with public leaders who work where decisions are made. One such strategic spot is hearings before legislative committees. Hearings play an important role in writing and reporting bills. Yet religious groups have often left a monopoly of such testimony to interest groups with weighty axes to grind. Having made public pronouncements, churchmen often neglect to focus on these key gatekeepers to legislative action. Carefully prepared testimony should persuasively present the most pertinent arguments and answer opposition claims. Any single presentation should be undergirded by facts including illustrations from experience, presented by one competent enough to answer questions. Those planning the presentation of one side of the case should give time to a good cross section of organizations and a good spread of supporting arguments. Groups unable to be represented personally may be allowed to present a written statement for the record.

This leads to a word about organizational resolutions in general. Individual opinion may be reinforced by the action of key organizations, particularly if the resolution is supplemented by other forms of action. Instead of remaining buried in the secretary's minutes, a resolution should be sent to the persons most concerned. It may be given additional impact if a congressman reads it into the *Congressional Record* or if copies are sent also to local political leaders. If the action is momentous enough to get into the public press, lawmakers may be reached through such publication, even if one incorporates only the kernel of a resolution in a letter to the editor. Clippings of all news coverage should be sent to the legislator. Since it is easy to say "aye" in a group meeting, resolutions by less prestigious organizations may not carry as much weight as would personal contacts. Therefore, all those who vote for a resolution should be encouraged to write individual letters as well. Unless organization members follow up in some such way, passing resolutions may become an inconsequential form of indoor entertainment.

Personal interviews with public officials are more available than we often think. Legislators, for example, can be seen not only in the capital city but between sessions in the offices they are likely to maintain in their home districts. The word "lobbying" carries a bad odor because we associate it with unworthy tactics or unethical motivations. It does not need to carry these connotations. In the sense of communicating with legislators, it is as much a part of the democratic process as is voting. For example, there can be no objection to personal interviews that try to persuade by presenting data that may help the congressman evaluate rival political claims.

Certain specific suggestions may be helpful to the amateur spokesman. (1) Make an appointment whenever possible. It is often acceptable to call a legislator off the "floor" to talk in the hall. If it is not possible to see the representative himself, talk to his assistant. (2) State views clearly and concisely, usually confining an interview to no more than two or three subjects. (3) Study in advance your representative's voting records and general attitudes. In order to speak most persuasively it is important to know the reaction you may expect and the probable limits of an official's readiness to move. (4) Master the important facts about the issues to be discussed, including the legislative status of any bills involved. Supply information of the kind that is likely to be genuinely helpful to the legislator's thinking and speaking. Be prepared to meet the most probable objections. (5) It is often well to visit in small groups as broadly representative as possible. In such cases, a leader should be selected as spokesman for the delegation. He will introduce other members, clearly identifying the groups they represent, and, in general, guide the discussion. In an individual interview, group stands can be presented by quoting positions taken by your church or other organizations. (6) Be positive, brief, constructive, and friendly. Show honest and deep conviction, but talk *with* instead of *to* the legislator. Try to understand his problems and to meet his individual objections rather than to "pressure" him. (7) Suggest some specific action to which the official might commit himself, such as voting or speaking for a bill or reading your resolution into the *Congressional Record.* (8) Leave with the person interviewed compilations of relevant data or a summary statement. (9) Notify local newspapers of the delegation's visit and send to your representative clippings of any news story that appears. Editors are more likely to provide publicity if there is something particularly timely or dramatic about the episode. (10) Follow up a visit with appropriate correspondence.

When citizens desire to persuade representatives, the aid of influential local persons may be enlisted, including ward or precinct captains, county or state party chairmen, prominent industrialists or civic leaders, and key persons in organizations well thought of by the legislator. Not only is their word directly important to the lawmaker; their expression of opinion also helps shape public sentiment. Another function which trusted lieutenants may perform is to transmit a particularly persuasive estimate of public opinion through the political grapevine.

Letter-writing is one of the most valuable political contacts in which the nonspecialist citizen can easily participate. Letters may be an elementary form of political action, yet this is an excellent place to begin. Letters are more effective than petitions, important as the latter may sometimes be. While petitions to parliamentary bodies have had a long and honorable history, their great weakness grows out of the ease of signing them. Politicians know that many persons thoughtlessly and without real conviction sign any petition thrust before them. Signatures on a petition should never be allowed to become a lazy substitute for individual letters.

Letters make possible a kind of town meeting by postage stamp. Such correspondence and the special-rate opinion telegrams now available are effective even if they are handled by a secretary, since the legislator gets a tally and report. Communications from home are one important way public officials gauge prevailing reactions. A congressman is more likely to take a courageous stand if mail is favorable. He may be discouraged from voting his support if his mail is adverse. Since this method is so easily available to all of us, a longer section of suggestions is justified.

1. Be original and sincere. Quite understandably, legislators pay more attention to letters if they are both numerous and spontaneous. If a flurry appears to be whipped up by a special-interest group, these letters are discounted as expressing less personal conviction. An Ohio senator received thousands of letters concerning railway legislation, each letter having the same mistake in regard to his middle initial. This was a clear symptom of an organized campaign. Several hundred telegrams in two days came to another senator, who later discovered that most of them had been sent without knowledge of the purported signers and had been charged to a single corporation's telephone. A few years ago senators from Massachusetts received telegrams opposing a particular Social Security action, all of them uniformly spelling "amendment" with a double *m*. Printed messages and form letters prepared by others are to be avoided. A person must show that he knows something about the subject and that he is acting to a great extent on his own initiative.

2. Be brief and specific. Brevity should still allow presentation of one or two reasons for a position. If possible, give the title or number of the bill to which you refer. Discuss only one subject in a single letter. Convictions on other subjects can be expressed in separate letters.

3. Ask a thoughtful question or two and request a reply. This should indicate a sincere interest in a congressman's views.

4. Feel free to write a reasonable number of successive letters on the same issue. New ideas or comments on your correspondent's replies may be sent later. If a letter is simply acknowledged without the legislator committing him-

self, the original question might be courteously restated. Do not become so obnoxious that your letters are heavily discounted. Yet, realize that the responsibility of citizenship is not fulfilled in one letter a year.

5. Maintain an unfailing courtesy along with the maximum possible appreciation. Abuse easily antagonizes. A scorching, threatening letter often does less damage in your own wastebasket than in a legislator's incoming mailbag. Commendation for favorable action should be as forthcoming as the disagreement that often follows unacceptable votes.

6. Learn something about your correspondent's characteristics and prejudices. Take them into account in phrasing communications.

7. Avoid "deathbed politics." Write early enough, while a bill is still in committee, or before a legislator has made up his mind. The White House staff is often interested in the immediate public response to a presidential speech before an organized lobbying campaign has time to develop. A telegram within six hours may have additional force. Keeping current on correspondence requires a legislative bulletin from agencies that provide this service, direction from a local church committee, or an alert reading of newspapers for significant developments.

8. Concentrate on your own representative. William Muehl in his *Politics for Christians* has suggested: "One of the first principles of successful political action is recognition of the fact that politicians are more apt to be influenced by an angry housewife from their own bailiwick than by a host of angels from the next town." Do not hesitate, however, to write key officials such as chairmen or members of legislative committees, majority and minority leaders, sponsors of bills, or executive officers, who ought to be more widely responsive.

If each of us felt that by writing one letter he could bring permanent peace to the world, he would drop this book and immediately write the letter. It is true that if enough of us write appropriate letters, we can get a policy that makes peace much more likely. Where is your stationery? It is part of the little man's equipment for social effectiveness.

Another major leisure-time vocation can be found in active membership in the political club or precinct organization of the party of your choice, or in those pressure groups which include a political purpose. While not all churchmen will find their calling here, in view of the importance of politics considerably more ought to be making this a secular ministry. To a great extent, politics is local and therefore accessible. Anyone can become active on the precinct or community-club level and by worthy participation begin to have a voice in party affairs. Kermit Eby used to say, "Bring up your parishioners to be precinct captains and the presidency will take care of itself." If we mean business about major public decisions, private Christian citizens in their individual capacities ought to recruit precinct workers with the same energy and conviction that we use in finding church school teachers or youth counselors.

Those not continuously active may become vigorous participants during specific campaigns, either as party workers or as independent supporters of a reform group interested in a particular issue. What appears from the outside to be a thrilling race may appear from the inside to be sheer drudgery—but so is the education of children or the launching of a satellite to the moon, if one does not keep an eye on the goal. Election activity begins far back with persuading qualified men to run. Numerous capable churchmen should remain open to the possibility of running for or accepting appointment to public office, not neglecting local school boards, city commissions, or civil service positions. Where states provide for them, primary elections are neglected only at our peril. These are often more important than the final contest since they are the narrow gates through which all candidates must pass. He who controls that gate can control the character of public officials. Since primaries are usually the most neglected of elections, this control can be exercised by a small political machine that manages to maintain a majority of the light vote.

In either primaries or final elections, the things that need to be done to ensure a victory celebration include getting citizens to register and getting voters to the polls. The electorate can be informed through our canvassing from door to door, distributing literature, making personal contacts with neighbors, or giving teas to introduce local candidates. Voting records are to be publicized, and questionnaires to candidates may be distributed. Money is to be raised to cover the large expenditures often necessary in modern campaigns. On election day there is transportation to organize, child care to provide, and poll watchers to be gotten. All this is a part of political literacy in our times.

Just as persons rather unanimously expect to get married or to find a job, so should they expect to become engaged in some aspect of politics. As a matter of course, all of us expect to prepare for other essential roles of a normal life. If in mass complexity we expect democratic civilization long to endure, the regular training of every child to maturity must include also political tactics.

At a critical time in Hebrew history, when the people remained unconcerned about Abimelech's bloody *coup d'état,* Jotham told this fable. The trees, said he, once searched for a king. They invited the olive tree, the fig tree, and the vine to rule over them, but each of them was preoccupied with fatness or sweetness or wine. Finally, in desperation they appealed to the bramble, but the price to be paid for lack of political responsibility was that fire should "come out of the bramble and devour the cedars of Lebanon" (Judg. 9:15). There are modern human versions of fatness or sweetness or wine—and of fire from the bramble.

6

Finding the Facts

DAVID LILIENTHAL once described the five members of the Atomic Energy Commission as "quintuplets in a quandary." A similar phrase could be applied to most of the population. Millions are now living with more facts and with greater bewilderment. Most of us know too much to remain comfortable but too little to be of any real help.

This is the day of the headline and the digest, the advertiser and the public relations consultant. We long for simple answers in small, sugarcoated capsules. A reading repertoire of novels and the sports page is the layman's equivalent of the professor's ivory tower. Our precise understanding of important issues remains as smoggy as a summer afternoon in Los Angeles. Even professional persons, who ought to know better, too often qualify for the description President Charles W. Eliot of Harvard applied to certain ministers who conduct their mental operations with "a maximum of intellectual frugality." To stop learning when one leaves school causes as serious a deficiency as would avoiding all fresh air or vitamins. After all, the man who *does not* read has no noticeable advantage over the man who *cannot* read.

A population that is sociologically illiterate is not equipped for twentieth-century living. A comic-book, picture-magazine mind becomes dangerous in a jet-propelled world. No man in his right mind would try to bring down a nuclear missile with a paper wad. Yet that is just what those are attempting who mismatch technological marvels with sociological ignorance. We throw instrument-crammed satellites around the moon and computerize our manufacturing. But when we get into repeated trouble in the Middle East, Far East, and various other points of the compass, we too often vote for political leaders because they have a comfortable television image.

Improvement of our social competence is a primary ethical obligation. Consecrated ignorance is not adequate service to God. We may be sensitive to human suffering but at the same time actually increase misery by uninformed ways of dealing with it. Love drives us beyond good intentions to secure whatever knowledge is necessary actually to serve persons. An incompetent driver can kill pedestrians very efficiently. Untutored parents can create juvenile delinquents very rapidly. Ignorance and folly may become more dangerous than are selfishness and malice, if benign men more easily gain public confidence in their false solutions.

Modern technology produces propaganda devices that could substitute mass manipulation for public education. Or without any ill will, simply carelessness or mediocrity in communication may prevent the high public competence now required. Illustrations are not hard to find. We trip over them everywhere. While this chapter was being written, newspaper headlines announced that "U.S. allies" supported further military escalation in Vietnam. Careful reading showed the support coming from those few lesser powers who were assisting us there, with no mention made of those major powers who are our "allies" in a considerably more significant sense, but who do not support a more militant Vietnam policy. The general impact of the article suggests a conclusion quite contrary to the actual situation. Even if one agrees with the policy being defended, one ought to demand a defensible defense.

Sometime ago an advertising campaign tried to prove that a certain breakfast cereal—let's call it X—stayed crisp longer than its leading competitors. The publicity was replete with references to "trained investigators," "watch in hand," visiting "more than 1,000 home kitchens." When cereal X and a competing brand were each put in a separate bowl, X was preferred an overwhelming number of times. Unfortunately, there was no indication of the number of times each of the several competing brands was used in the second bowl, nor were there any comparative scores for each brand. It would have been statistically possible, on the basis of information provided, for cereal X to have been one of the worst of all the brands, if the crisper competitors had been placed in the second bowl less often than the soggier competitors. Statistics can bear the same relationship to some publications that the chaplain bears in occasional legislative assemblies, to provide a façade of respectability to whatever would have taken place anyway. Their significance is ceremonial rather than scientific.

Brief slogans are particularly slippery. They easily stampede us into action on the basis of immediate reflexes instead of careful reflection. The printed handouts may proclaim, "The voluntary way is the American way." Perhaps it is and then again perhaps it isn't. The voluntary way is the American way for cutting lawns, not for sending children to school. It is for the selection of one's church, but not for the selection of speed on the highway. There is considerable difference between the purely voluntary way and the democratic way. Or bumper stickers may protest, "Please, Uncle Sam, I would rather do it myself." An appropriate response would be, "What do you plan to use for science laboratories or football stadiums?" Would we really rather educate our own children in our living rooms or provide protection against aggression by totalitarian nations with a musket hung over the fireplace? Again, some things we should do for ourselves; others we should not. Without an analysis of the activity at issue the slogan provides no illumination whatsoever. Many slogans, including those which have a habit of appearing on billboards at election time, are an insult to public intelligence. They are about as conclusively relevant to the matter under discussion as the bathing beauties draped over the hood in the automobile advertisements are related to the performance of the motor under the hood. Or they may be as deceptive as the smiling television announcer who talks about the taste of the cigarette without any mention of the health hazards tied into the sale.

Even with the best of intentions, the printed page or the spoken word always involves some selectivity. Both writers and readers might share the complaint attributed to a high school girl: "It's not that I don't like current events. It's just that there have been so many of them lately." No newspaper can print all the news, and no book or speaker can include all the important material on a subject. If newspapers printed on any one day an account of all plants not on strike or all couples not suing for divorce, they would quickly exhaust available newsprint. Editorializing takes place by what the editor drops into his wastebasket. Even when media of mass communication tell the truth, they cannot tell the whole truth.

Selectivity also enters into the comparative emphasis given to items. There is a tyranny about the front page. Items featured there are given importance beyond those buried on back pages. A newspaper wishing to discredit a city administration can manufacture the appearance of a crime wave at any time by publishing details of arrests that would not otherwise be mentioned, or by moving more crime news into a position of prominence in the paper.

"Engineering of consent" becomes especially serious with a growing monopoly in the means of mass communication. The democratic principle of a free and open encounter of ideas requires a variety of agencies of expression. Now certain points of view are less readily available because of the disappearance of competing newspapers or the greater cost of access to the mass media. At the same time that these media have become more effective, they have also become more costly. Not every man with a fact or an idea can buy television time. The air waves tend disproportionately to be restricted to those who have been treated kindly enough by the *status quo* that they have the necessary funds. These beneficiaries of things as they are may also be less likely to see the need for improving existing conditions. This becomes a source of an important conservative bias in our society, a way of slowing down progress on basic matters.

Also because mass media aim at maximum attention there is a temptation to reflect the existing interests, tastes, and prejudices of the population. A "least common denominator" approach may most easily attract the largest audience and the highest advertising revenue, but it does not present the widest spectrum of unpopular truth. It is hazardous, therefore, to derive one's social philosophy entirely from mass circulation media. Some of the most insidious effects result from incidental matters seen as a matter of course. The luxury of homes portrayed in the movies deepens our identification of status with opulence, in spite of world poverty. The fact that executives in television scripts are overwhelmingly business and professional men and not labor leaders, white and not Negro, is not the best possible design for objectivity in industrial or race relations.

Not only public schools but also churches should teach people how to read. Public-spirited agencies need to nurture a healthy skepticism concerning the printed page and television screen, showing us how to protect ourselves against propaganda and how to build the indispensable foundation of facts.

The first lesson to be learned is the need for a basic background. Instead of evaluating each statement about a newly emerging problem in complete isolation, we ought to interpret it in the light of the most we already know about Christian ethics and social science. The more such resources we have, the easier it will be to detect lurking fallacies or dangerous distortions. Formal education should have gotten us off to a head start here, especially if the schools we attended encouraged full exploration of different points of view. Continuing reading and education as adults can supplement and update our background. Church school curricula can help a great deal, both in theological and sociological dimensions for decision.

There is no substitute for an investment of time in such serious study. On the other hand, this is a manageable matter. To maintain the necessary level of citizen competence the man on the street does not need to read detailed historical studies or sociological analyses that are required by scholars and administrative specialists. To vote on general policy the citizen does need to know the essential nature of major problems, important alternative solutions being suggested, and significant consequences of each of these alternatives. This takes more serious study and greater concentration on important matters than most of us are accustomed to. But it is entirely possible for literate persons, especially if we rescue time for more important matters by cutting the irrelevant and the trivial out of our schedules. No man in his right mind should spend more than a few minutes on the average daily newspaper. He needs to turn to more thoughtful articles, lectures, pamphlets, or books.

A second commandment to observe is, Select your sources. Stop gulping down everything in print as though it were the gospel. Turn to as objective a group of materials as it is possible to find. As we serve the God of truth, we are bound to try to clear away the distortions of human bias. About every doctrine or speech that bids for our attention we need to raise the same kind of discriminating test questions that the historian would ask. Who is making the statement? Is he in a position to know? What ability or access to the facts does he have? What proof is offered? Is it adequate? What bias does the author represent? Why did he write this? Whose axe is being ground? What propaganda devices are being used? What selectivity and slant are given the material?

Among comparatively disinterested sources are many scholars and competent churchmen. While not every professor or religious researcher is a paragon of objectivity, there are experts in academic and ecclesiastical circles who do investigate beyond superficial materials, and who have comparatively little personal stake in even the most controversial issues. Standard textbooks or journals are usually good sources. Popular treatments such as the Public Affairs Pamphlets may be profound as well as easily understood. Denominational or ecumenical journals include much good material. Lectures by competent people can be increasingly brought to local congregations.

Lack of prejudice is entirely a matter of degree. Some materials are more reliable than others, but every source is somewhat biased. For this reason the most practically useful advice that can normally be given is that we balance our reading. Usually we cannot rely on a single source of information. We need to read both sides—or all four sides!

Careful attention includes checking our own present conclusions against opposing convictions. Social psychologists make much of the concepts of selective attention and selective interpretation. We tend to read only what we already agree with or to read our own desired meanings into material that presents a different position. Thus we stunt any further growth and mire even farther down into our existing prejudices. It has been suggested that we should read for information, inspiration, and irritation. The last purpose is often overlooked, yet the first purpose, information, can scarcely be achieved without it. When we read the headlines announcing a new strike, our immediate reaction is likely to curse either labor or management, depending on our general sympathies, without getting the facts about this particular situation. We had bet-

ter restrain our spontaneous curses until we have studied
the case for the opposition.

Balance requires exposure to both the conservative and
the liberal points of view. Apparently as a population we
do not do well at this, since circulation figures for essentially conservative periodicals are considerably larger than
those of publications that advocate more thoroughgoing
change. This is understandable in view of our general desire to be confirmed in the opinions we now hold. Yet it is
not the best path to objective understanding. To balance
our biases, most of us must read more than the popular
press. This is not because the liberal position in any in-
stance is necessarily right, but simply because a conclusion
on either side should rest on an understanding of the other
side. Some of us who have concentrated unduly on publications criticizing things as they are need also to read
material defending the existing situation. Reading the releases of the AFL-CIO as well as of the National Association of Manufacturers is necessary for the deepest insight.
We need to listen to businessmen and labor leaders, to
reform and antireform groups. Republicans and Demo-
crats should read each other's platforms and speeches.
Many feel that if they read *Reader's Digest* or *U.S. News
& World Report,* they should also read *The Nation* or *The
New Republic*—and vice versa.

In analyzing divergent sources, every citizen needs to
remember that the truth does not necessarily lie halfway
between the two. We cannot unite heaven and hell "by
combining the best features of both." On lesser contrasts
also, halving the difference is seldom a mature method.
Not all "facts" are born free and equal. Rival contentions
have to be evaluated and truth claims interpreted. Is there
internal consistency within a position? Which arguments
presented are most sound and most important? How does
each correct the other? What agreements appear? What
factors are likely to underlie disagreement? Can points
of disagreement be checked against reasonably objective

sources? By mixing such intellectual labor with publicity materials, we are likely to get nearer the truth than if we allow to any one side a monopoly of expression.

Weighing two sides is easier when one lists pro and con arguments under the most important subissues. For example, in studying the death penalty, one may conclude that the two sides disagree on such questions as: Does the death penalty deter crime? Does it brutalize society? Is it applied disproportionately to racial or lower-class groups? Are there better ways for protecting the public? Under each of these questions the most relevant evidence presented by the contending disputants can be listed, and some conclusions reached about where the preponderance of evidence falls. This is more than adding up the number of arguments on each side or being impressed by multiplication of statements saying essentially the same thing in different ways. This requires evaluating the quality of arguments and the comparative importance of subissues.

Any evaluation of opposite positions always involves ethical presuppositions. As was pointed out in a previous chapter, the social sciences help us understand issues, list alternatives, and describe the consequences of each. Religious faith provides a theological view of reality and moral guidelines in the light of which options are to be judged. Accumulating the immediate facts about current problems is never enough. This remains a shallow pastime unless it is given a context of deeper meaning. Things are not always what they first seem to be. Paul Tillich speaks of a "sociology of depth" that sees profound realities beneath surface experiences and plunges finally to God as the ultimate depth of history. Such an inclusive perspective involves adding values to descriptive facts and a view of the whole to isolated fragments. The Christian makes a particularly valuable contribution to social decision because he continuously recalls which goals really count and what life is all about.

From such a marriage of the theological and sociological

there should be born a social philosophy maximizing Christian values in a particular time and place in history. As a result of the most objective analysis of which we are capable, we will come out at a particular point on the spectrum of public opinion that runs from the radical on the left through the liberal and conservative to the reactionary on the right. Equally sincere Christians on controversial matters that are hard to resolve may not stop at the same point. The same person may not come down at the same place on the general spectrum on different issues. Yet some general things can be said that may be helpful to the citizen who would inform his decisions by the Christian faith.

A person has already made a substantial beginning in his general orientation when he recognizes that the claim of God is superior to the commands or customs of men and that love requires needs of neighbors to be given priority over comforts for the self. The general objectives for social decision are then clear. Ideologies and social programs are to be tested by whether or not they serve human need, rather than the formulations of the past being rigidly perpetuated no matter how much suffering they cause in the present.

Insofar as possible, we try to see things from the standpoint of those with the most desperate needs. The Christian faces in this direction when he looks at all definitions of situations, arguments pro and con, and proposals for action. It makes a good deal of difference whose shoes one is standing in when he views a situation. Each of us has seen things only from a limited perspective. Most readers of these lines are likely to be to some extent prisoners of a middle-class environment. Our closest associates reflect these same interests. Our experiences are highly selective. Our attention has been shielded from suffering in the slums or in Africa. We have tended to shove around a limited number of old ideas, as we do trunks and dress forms in an attic, and we have called this thinking. Again and again major changes in basic philosophy have come to conventional, satisfied citizens, content with compromise and accustomed to apathy, when they had an eye-opening contact with desperate human need. This is the reason "go and see" trips are so important in any religious education program. Since many situations of need are not immediately accessible, we also need dramatic encounters through books, movies, and creative imagination.

If a man of goodwill is aware of reality, he will always have a program for the underdog. The privileged also have serious needs, but they have more resources and more people concerned about them. Most of us more easily identify with them. It is the situation we do not see that we must make the greatest effort to know. The immediately obvious is not enough to build conclusions on. It is no accident, therefore, that the Bible should stress our obligations to the poor and needy. This hard word must be spoken to us also. The Christian has no alternative except to identify himself unequivocally with the neglected, the oppressed, and the underprivileged.

As a second general observation, in dealing with the hurts of men, the Christian will be suspicious of the extreme positions of the radical and the reactionary. The first of these would advocate sudden, revolutionary, and perhaps violent change while the last would drastically turn back the clock of history to a past age. On public issues both of these are normally too destructive and in the long run even self-defeating. Neanderthal men do rather regularly crawl out of their caves every morning to report to work in the halls of Congress or the boardrooms of corporations and labor unions. We ought vigorously to object to such antiquarian antics. At the same time we ought to oppose those who would have futuristic spacemen pile out of their alien flying saucers to capture our cities and impose a utopian civilization appropriate only to some never-never land. Some among us guard the past too much and prepare for the future too little. Others regard the past too little and thereby endanger the future too much.

Extremists on both the left and the right tend to become totalitarian and to endanger a society of freedom and justice. The extremist on the right lives in the present as though it were the past unaware that the future has already surrounded him. Before they can do too much damage, as Adlai Stevenson suggested, they need to be carried kicking and screaming into the twentieth century. Extremists on the left are so eager for the future that they disrupt too many values from the past and make the present a vast wasteland. The only way to beat such a group is to beat them to it, proving that a vigorous rapid program of responsible peaceful change can more certainly achieve their ideal goals than can a destructively revolutionary program. If we cannot soon enough demonstrate the resources of democracy for dealing with suffering and need, the extremists on the left will eventually inherit the earth. The spirit of man will not permanently endure tragic injustice or halfhearted approaches to cruel and long-continued suffering.

This leads to a third general observation. In an imperfect society some change is always necessary. If we reject the extremes of the radical and the reactionary, our choice is to be made between responsible "liberalism" and dynamic "conservatism." Insofar as they are acceptable, both of these need to be committed to improvement and therefore to change. The differences between them will then arise at the point of rapidity or type of change. In a dynamic society we cannot hold things completely as they are. A technological invention in one area of life inevitably requires improvements in other areas. On such matters unless we take a well-considered step forward, we will inevitably take a disastrous step backward.

In a time of rapid social change such as the present, what was once conservative quickly becomes reactionary and what was once liberal rapidly becomes conservative. Not too many years ago it was considered radical to advocate international organization. Then it became the position of the thoroughgoing liberal. Now it has become a conservative position since the United States is a member of the United Nations and a vast majority of the American people according to public-opinion polls feel that we should retain our membership. The issue now is in what respects and how rapidly the United Nations should be strengthened.

Only by perpetual discontent with the present do we contribute to the future. Progress of necessity requires giving up something old in favor of something new. When automobiles are introduced, buggies are stored in the barn. Logically this is conclusive. Psychologically it is hard to accept because of the inflexibilities of custom and habit. Any adequate social philosophy must break through these confining walls to say what formerly was not being said.

This point is more easily seen in technological matters. Both scientific discovery and industrial progress need persons who do not have the slightest suspicion anywhere in the back of their heads that there is anything in this world that is as good as it might be. That is the pioneering spirit that has made our civilization great. At their best, science and industry, and politics too, put money and time into finding fault with existing processes and products in order that something better might be invented.

Thomas Huxley suggested that Alexander Pope's declaration, "Whatever is, is right," ought to be emblazoned in letters of mud over all the pigsties of the world. In an imperfect world it is easier to conclude that whatever is, is somewhat wrong. The requirement of God judges every act of man and goes far beyond our present attainment. John U. Nef, professor of economic history at The University of Chicago, once pointed out that legally we consider a man innocent until he is proved guilty, but that morally "none of the major actions of men in our time can be justified until they are proved right. Before the justice of *man* all should claim a presumption of innocence. Be-

fore the justice of *God* all have a duty to presume that they
are guilty." The walls of habit easily become the tomb of
the soul, and the crust of custom frequently covers the
grave of society. The resources of the past are properly
used to go beyond the past. Appropriately, on the National
Archives Building in Washington appears the inscription,
"What's past is prologue." We dare never allow the clear
stream of contemporary insight to be absorbed into the
dreary desert of tradition.

A fourth guideline grows out of the third. Like society
as a whole, each of us individually needs continuously to
change his social convictions in order to incorporate novel
conclusions and superior insights. This ought to come as
no surprise to the Christian, who has sworn allegiance to
a God whose perfection reveals as imperfect the best
thought of finite man. We are therefore always called to
some conversion of our convictions, lest we defend what
God opposes and attack what God champions. We commit
the sin of pride when we resist any revision of our present
conclusions.

In spite of this, some partisans of an ideal have been
crusaders with closed minds, dogmatically defending a
position that they refuse to review. Thus they repeat on a
new level the same sort of static situation against which
they originally rebelled. The most creative person is a participant in a continuous quest; he is always eager for new
light. At the same time, he knows that he must act on the
basis of such insight as he has until decisive new evidence
appears. He will not erratically flit from position to position. Yet he will also know that if we believe the same
things now that we believed ten years ago, we undoubtedly
need some fresh study. Since it is now estimated that all
human knowledge doubles in six or seven years, we can
expect part of our detailed notions to become regularly
outmoded.

Resistance to personal change is a temptation to older
people who think they have done enough homework

through a lifetime, yet the social situation keeps changing, not at the same speed it always did, but at an accelerating rate. It is also a peculiar temptation to those who win worldly success that they permanently adopt the convictions that accompanied their triumph. All of us face some form of the same temptation to stifle continuous curiosity and to yield to creeping conformity to cultural pressure.

These four guidelines to a constructive social philosophy invite us to search for the general orientation that in a given historical epoch best serves the needs of mankind. It is possible to do this without becoming either fanatical through oversimplification or immobilized by complexity. This process of perfecting a general social philosophy may be illustrated in terms of the basic domestic issue facing us today. Our orientation on this underlying principle shapes our conclusions on many of the controversial proposals constantly emerging for debate.

Sometimes called the central issue in political science is the question of individual freedom versus group control. The form of the question especially pertinent now is the extent to which economic activities and services should be regulated or provided by group action through the state. One extreme on this matter is political totalitarianism, involving a highly centralized control of almost every aspect of life. This we reject because of its denial of freedom and also in the long run its threat to order. The other extreme is anarchy, or the system that allows every man to do what is right in his own eyes without external restraint. At first sight this has a strong appeal. It would appear at least to provide for maximum liberty, but when we recall the nature of man, his propensity to evil by serving his own interest, we begin to have second thoughts. In a completely unregulated situation, it is not long before the strongest or the most unscrupulous or the most capable or the most fortunate begin to gather disproportionate power to themselves and to dominate others. If every man were completely altruistic and completely wise, a system of anarchy might be defended; but in the existing world, when anarchy is attempted, it is transformed into its precise opposite, autocracy, or the control by the few.

This process was illustrated in the frontier community before the advent of law and order. Soon the man with the fastest draw and the most accurate aim became the law. Others acted freely only at his sufferance. This intolerable condition was cured by the introduction of democracy and the election of a sheriff. Similar consequences have historically followed the attempt to maintain complete freedom in economic life. The overall trend has been for many small independent businesses to be superseded by near monopolies who make the decisions for that section of the economy. Again to safeguard both freedom and justice, we have found it necessary to establish regulatory commissions or to pass laws to protect the common interests.

This elementary lesson in political science is often forgotten when a controversial law is being debated. Then it is often argued that the passage of any regulation, especially in the economic area, is an undesirable limitation of freedom. With respect to the population as a whole, exactly the opposite may be the case. Maximum freedom is found in a government of wise laws. The question is never one of avoiding law; it is, rather, one of avoiding unnecessary or ill-advised laws. Whenever men live in groups, regulation by society is necessary all the way from speed limits to prohibiting private ownership of nuclear bombs. Avoiding the extremes of anarchy and totalitarianism, and somewhere in the range of continuous democratic change, those committed to a better meeting of human needs will find their program. The questions that divide them become matters of content and timing. What specific actions are desirable? How soon should they be taken?

When this same range of choice is put in its economic context, the extremes become a completely unregulated laissez-faire individualism on the one hand and economic collectivism on the other. For reasons similar to those already outlined, the major democratic nations, including our own, have rejected these opposite poles. The area within which public decisions are being made is that of a mixed economy including private interests, public regulation or enterprise, and in many countries a sizable consumers cooperative sector. The issue then becomes in what proportion these various elements are to be combined. It is here that liberals and conservatives divide. Conservatives tend to support an arrangement about as we have it now with minor modifications. They feel that rather large doses of free enterprise can best meet the problems of poverty, race discrimination, urban life, education, and leisure that now confront us. The liberal, seeking more rapid change and prepared to make more thoroughgoing modifications, would in our society also retain privately-owned economic enterprise as the chief ingredient in his mix. However, he feels it important to turn more frequently to group action through government to express the common purpose in coordinated ways.

On choices such as these, the Christian will expect continuously to grow personally if he is to be creative socially. Diligent about gathering facts objectively and incorporating them coherently into a basic social philosophy, he will be guided by a concern for man that is deepened by religious dimensions. Following faithfully what he sees as the movement of God, he will base his life on an ethics for the future that goes beyond even conventional wisdom and prestigious customs. So in these best and worst of times, he can make a contribution to outcomes as exciting as the Magna Carta, the industrial revolution, or the Protestant Reformation—or perhaps, in an era of accelerating change, to all three rolled into one.

7

Church Resources
for Churchmen's Witness

ONE of the most striking illustrations in Harvey Cox's *The Secular City* is the account of a group of World Council of Churches leaders returning from a Christian youth conference in Africa. In spite of the large attendance at the conference they agreed that in ten years most young Africans would have cut all ties with the church. The present teachings of the church, they felt, were simply not related to the issues faced by African young people moving from a tribal to a technopolitan civilization.

If one searched for the major influences now determining the destiny of mankind, one would have to place the church rather far down the list even though it is supposed to be the custodian of God's revelation essential to man's salvation. At the moment, the future of the world is more largely being shaped by military establishments, science and technology, conflicting economic systems, the rise of new nations, urbanization, or the population explosion. The church has been nudged off to the side of modern history. Or perhaps confused by rapid change, or fearing possible opposition, it has itself wandered off to a protected isolation.

Deliverance for both church and society requires a renewal within the church considerably more radical than even most church leaders realize. The concept of churchmen undertaking a vast invasion of culture in novel ways has more drastic implications for the church itself than we imagine. It is not enough to provide the same, only more of it, nor to make superficial improvements of the old. It is much too late for that. Just as individual churchmen need a notable change in their typical pattern of life, so also the church must profoundly change, or its apostasy will unavoidably be followed by its decline. Even as a new generation of laymen will demand these alterations in their church, so will a renewed church support a new breed of laymen. There are certain resources of this kind which churchmen have a right to expect from their church.

The first such ecclesiastical response is that the church will more clearly establish the contemporary relevance of a historical religion. Modern, scientific, technological man is functionally oriented, insisting on evaluating any organization or program by its contribution to accepted goals. Rightly or wrongly, he sees the church as traditional, protecting ancient ways regardless of their appropriateness to the present. Modern man looks to the future for the golden age, after more inventions have been made. The church often seems to see perfection in the past, in the days of Jesus and the early church. Contemporary man expects the most recent books to be more reliable since they have had the advantage of cumulative research, and he also suspects the church to be the one major institution in society where antiquity is an argument for truth. Such modernity can be exaggerated, overlooking our roots in the past. Yet modern man is right in insisting that learnings from the past have no important human significance unless they help us shape a better future. We should rejoice whenever men rebel against any church that majors in history and minors in psychology and sociology, at the same time that we should also rebel against the opposite error. The first is a much more common mistake of the church today. Insofar as the church is more interested in or more competent about bygone topics than about contemporary issues, it is stumbling over its own feet, building obstacles in its own path, and standing as a barrier between God and man.

We have so long spoken on so many questions no one was asking that many persons no longer expect from the church any word on the issues that really bother them, such as nuclear threat, business competition, or sex drives. To a certain extent we have built a constituency that is satisfied with irrelevancy. Traditionalists in the congregation mold ministers in their own image, while all the time "outsiders" are being driven farther away from the church. What we do to warm the hearts of "insiders" frequently contributes to the further alienation of "outsiders." All one has to do to understand why the church has no wider appeal is to sit in some adult classes. Discussion often goes into minute detail about ancient matters. At the same time nothing except the most extreme generalizations suggests that the Christian faith makes any difference on significant modern problems. We really need to decide whether this will be the last generation to fill our sanctuaries. This relates not only to whether or not mortgages will be paid off, but much more important, to whether the gospel will be shared with the world. This matter is as serious as all that.

There is little question but that the new generation increasingly anticipates that if a person entered a church, he would be met by antiquated liturgy, archaic words, and social irrelevance. This is a caricature of the church. Yet there is a basis for it. Greatly to alter the image means considerably to change the reality that the image reflects.

Laymen have a right to resent being treated as though they were Corinthians or Romans. They have come from the horse and buggy to space flights in a single generation. They can no longer be reached as though they were peasants in a preindustrial society or pioneers on a frontier instead of units in a mass urban society. The church still frequently speaks about work and vocation essentially as it did in an agricultural and handicraft society. The Bible uses much rural imagery — vineyards, lands, and fields of grain. This has less meaning to urban man who is at home with monorails, computers, and weightlessness in space. Unless we translate the Bible, it becomes a strange and alien document with a theological and ethical message seemingly appropriate only to a past age. The care of God then seems to be experienced only in green fields beside "still waters" and not on the "turf" of slum gangland. The story of David and Bathsheba has no advantage over some contemporary secular literature as an illustration of adultery. It may indeed have certain disadvantages, since it includes less psychological insight into the complexity of causes and seems to be so historically distant from us.

There is a "scandal" about the gospel that cannot be avoided. Its ethical imperative and fundamental call to faith will always seem a heavy burden to the libertine and the faithless. The church by its own incompetence should not be adding unnecessary burdens of meaningless requirements. To do so is to repeat the sin of the scribes and Pharisees who "bind heavy burdens, hard to bear, and lay them on men's shoulders; but they themselves will not move them with their finger" (Matt. 23:4).

This is particularly tragic because it is so unnecessary. The great historical foundations of the Christian faith do have fundamental meaning in modern terms. Our message is both timeless and timely. We do look to the future with hopeful expectation of a new age. The Christian faith can be communicated in terms that are the more effective because they are the more meaningful. The Holy Spirit speaks in ways fitted to each unique culture. God's transforming power is evident not only on Mt. Carmel or Calvary but also at Nicaea and Wittenberg, and in the frontier camp meeting and the antislavery crusade, and now again in a caucus of the concerned during a modern political convention, and to a lonely businessman in prayer before a crucial decision.

An adequately modern approach means no less empha-

sis on the great historical themes that are fundamental
to our faith. It does mean considerably less preoccupation
with nonessential embellishments of church programs in
order that, within the limits of time, energy, and other
resources, a comparatively greater emphasis can be placed
on the contemporary. Our aim is dynamic balance between historic faith and modern life. In no other way is
vital religion possible. If we have been off-balance on one
foot, we regain our balance only by shifting some weight
to the other foot. There is no way of avoiding this, painful
as it may sometimes be.

The prevailing image of the church must be radically
revamped at this point. On existing problems and potentialities the church has yet to prove that as a body, apart
from its leaders, it is alert, concerned, knowledgeable,
and active. A survey quoted in Chapter 3 showed that
most businessmen felt that they were not getting enough
help from the church. The same survey also indicated
that these businessmen would welcome help from their
ministers if they were convinced that the clergy knew
what they were talking about. To quote the report, "The
welcome which businessmen give to clerical advice is
directly proportional to the amount of knowledge that the
individual clergyman has about business." Political leaders
are not impressed by vague idealism apart from sound
arguments about specific bills. There is no substitute for
relating theology to the existing world by concrete work
on practical issues. It is necessary to break out of churchly
language into the idiom of the job and childhood and
the leisure world. This is the way it is with the Christian
faith. The church cannot remain bound to old forms
or formulations at the cost of silence on the present situation. Since our technopolitan culture is so much different
from the past, survival of the Christian witness depends
upon a major reworking comparable to the contribution
of theological giants in relationship to Greek philosophy,
the Roman world, the industrial revolution, or conditions

on the frontier. Henry Ward Beecher once began a sermon by saying, "If the sexton finds anyone asleep in my audience this morning, let him come up and wake me up." This applies to the church as well as to preachers. If modern man is finding the Christian faith less meaningful, it is time to shake the church out of its slumber. In times of accelerating change in other areas, movement toward new ecclesiastical emphases must also become more rapid.

A second contribution that a churchman has the right to expect from his church is training for witness at the outposts, the places at which the layman finds himself and where he is therefore called to work. The church exists not to extract people from the world but to inject revolutionary leaders back into it. A witnessing servant church must carefully equip its members for witness and servanthood. Our traditional curriculum gets off to a good start here insofar as it places a general emphasis on the service of God in the world of men, but it quickly breaks down when it needs to become specific about supporting theory and social skills. Therefore, one of the major illusions of our time is that ministers think that their words on Sunday have any significant influence on what their parishioners do on Monday.

In perplexing times laymen should know more about the Bible and theology than they have in the past. At the same time they ought not place such an emphasis on these subjects that no time is left for the understanding and skills necessary to contemporary citizenship. Fortunately, such double learning is possible by eliminating pedantic details formerly stressed, which both crowded out contemporary meanings and confused traditional materials. Sound education always involves concentration on major matters, which produce real insight, rather than on minor details, which obscure a view of the whole.

In Bible study, for example, laymen often feel guilty about the wrong things. They see themselves as inferior because they cannot pass tests on the details of Hebrew history, the differences between Biblical sources, or outlines of content of specific books. Let us be honest about it. It is a waste of time to master some intricacies about the Bible. Reading the Bible from cover to cover is not an exercise to be recommended. The time has come to say right out loud that the attempt to have laymen learn tiny items about the Bible may actually conceal the central message of Scripture. Such obscurantism should be taken out of the church school curriculum.

We were actually aided in our Biblical study when, as a result of the scientific revolution, we concluded that the Bible was not a book of science. On matters such as evolution we rightly turned to scientific textbooks, while we went to Scripture for the much more important matter of religious interpretation of Creation. Now we are also realizing that the Bible was never a textbook of systematic theology. Here also we must turn to other sources, while we concentrate in the Bible on those basic insights from which theologies can be constructed. So likewise we now need to see that the Bible is not an ethical rule book. In an index or concordance, words such as nuclear weapons, unemployment insurance, Medicare, or fair housing do not appear. Rather, the ethical contribution of the Bible is made in its general theological orientation and in its norms and guidelines for moral choice. It is this which we ought to master. At these points we need a great new resurgence of interest in Scriptural truth. When we do this the Bible may recover the central place that it deserves to have. It has come to have less importance in our culture partly because we have placed the wrong kind of emphasis upon it. This is like expecting a wonder drug to cure everything and then when it fails on some things, letting it lapse into disuse on everything. More popular terminology would refer to this as throwing out the baby with the bath. Utterly unanticipated new life is available to us if we use the Bible in ways that are true to its own nature.

We often face a similar problem with respect to theology. Serious study of this field is sometimes hindered by theologians who use up many pages elaborating answers to questions no one is concerned about. Therefore they repel their readers. These hairsplitting details are the present-day equivalent of medieval debates about the number of angels who might occupy the head of a pin. They are tithing "mint and dill and cummin" and neglecting "the weightier matters of the law, justice and mercy and faith" (Matt. 23:23). Thus we withdraw from humanity and alienate thoughtful contemporaries. This is one way of contributing to the problem instead of to the solution. If laymen spend time on such matters, we shall have a less learned and a less competent membership. Fastidiousness about less important theological niceties may block social commitment and nourish apathy toward human evils. A favorite device of propagandists after all is to keep people so busy with less important side issues that they pay no attention to main issues. Any practicing physician who devoted his time to studying differences between the human skeleton and the skeleton of the horse would be less scholarly and well trained than the doctor who invested available time in studying the latest findings on bone diseases.

Whatever the comparable necessities of the laity are, we have a right to expect that the church will effectively deal with them. This is true not only in the area of intellectual mastery but also in the acquisition of skills for active participation in community affairs. These skills require a competence considerably beyond common sense as we move within modern problems and power relationships. A wide variety of new materials from the behavioral sciences must be introduced for any adequate understanding of religion and for proficiency in lay action in the world. As we insist upon using the best techniques in church hospitals or colleges, so we should also settle for no less in the work which we expect adults in general to do. The findings of social psychology and community organization and public-opinion research should find a considerably larger place in the curricula of church school classes or short-term intensive training groups. For Christians committed to witness on the job and in the community just as continuous and intensive "in-service training" should be provided as is made available for church school teachers through their departmental meetings, workshops, or laboratory schools. If the laborer is worthy of his hire, he is also entitled to his tools.

A third reasonable expectation that laymen might have is that their church in its own practice provide supporting structure and projects for expression of a ministry to industry, community, and politics. An organizational channel is necessary for this as for any other social function. Those are sociologically naïve who are now suggesting that the church should become largely invisible, being engaged in silent, unobtrusive service to the world. This is a recipe for dissolution of the fellowship and defeat for its social witness. How can a reform movement or reformation be lost to view? If we are sociologically sophisticated about requirements for change in mass society, we must insist that the church be conspicuous in institutional leadership.

The church should become one of the pressure groups in society through which its members may act. A layman interested in removing immoral practices within his profession should have available in his denomination or council of churches an organized group of Christians in that profession through which to begin working. Any churchman concerned about controversial issues such as smog in the lungs, or drugs in the brains of the populace, has a right to expect an established social-action group in the church that might vote to take up his cause. Such a social-action unit would already have accumulated a great deal of experience and would have established contacts with legislators and government officials. A single layman working for a reform compounds his strength as he finds within his church an enabling fellowship or an organized body of supporters.

Those church members who develop a new concern ought to find projects sponsored by their church in which they can enlist. It is as serious an omission not to have a letter-writing campaign or political-action program going for such newly won recruits as it is not to have a Bible on hand when the high school class wants to look up a passage. As a matter of fact, the former experience might occasionally prove more life-changing (depending on what the project was) than the latter (depending on what the passage was)!

We quite regularly do terrible things to fellow church members when we do not provide action projects through which to express ideological convictions. Through worship or study classes we bring persons to a high degree of commitment. Then we provide no channels through which this existential decision can be acted out. We substitute knowing about a problem for doing something about it. Parishioners are then following the example of their church when, having read about the world in the evening newspaper, they simply go to bed. Churchmen in suspended animation who keep their good intentions in cold storage, find that their resolutions putrefy. Such persons are too delicate citizens for a dangerous world. By their failure to do good they actually strengthen evil. This is a very respectable but also an extremely potent social narcotic. Even worse, it is a very efficient way of betraying the battle to the enemy. By encouraging conviction without action we contribute to moral schizophrenia, a church-sanctioned split between being and doing. By its own example the church as a reference group is quite effectively teaching that the expression of commitment is not important. This is utterly foreign to our basic theology. This encourages a particularly virulent type of immorality. It is a form of insincerity in which outer conduct and inner conviction do not coincide. Such a disease incapacitates one for the Christian life.

In addition to supporting laymen with church structures and projects, the congregation's witness includes also the testimony of its own economic and social practices. What we are as a church often speaks more loudly than our press releases. Church leaders may offer to help businessmen in dealing with their vocational dilemmas. The church also teaches through its own handling of similar dilemmas. No degree of eloquence for a fair wage can make up for the low wages paid to the church janitor. The public can be forgiven for not heeding our injunction to racial integration so long as the congregation remains segregated. Such matters are not only ways of witness or of supporting conscientious laymen. They are also tests of the spiritual maturity of the congregation.

Suppose that the church introduced ritual adultery as part of its worship service. During the prelude each adult might have sex relations with the nearest person of the opposite sex who was not his spouse. Or suppose that instead of the morning offering, worshipers slipped out to a side room to place their bets with a gambling syndicate hired to run the Sunday sweepstakes, with a percentage covering the church budget. We should be immediately horrified by such practices and conclude that this was not a Christian church but rather a pagan temple. But suppose that during the organ prelude ushers were stationed on the steps of the sanctuary to keep Negroes from entering. Or perhaps the governing board of the church regularly enforced policies that kept out speakers on "controversial" subjects. Or suppose this congregation built for itself a great cathedral ostentatious in its ornamentation while in other lands Christians without any shelter worshiped in the rain under the trees. Or suppose that ministers and laymen simply spent most of their time on lesser things and devoted little energy to crucial problems of world peace or economic justice. Which ought to be considered worse—ritual adultery and lottery financing, or some of these latter examples, which actually exist as widespread practices? In terms of the extensive evil of the total consequences involved, some of the latter practices may be even worse than the former. Just as we repudiate the former with all that is holy within us, so should we react with equal vehemence to the latter.

In days that are decisively different, when both promise and peril are highly accelerated, the church badly needs to rearrange its order of priorities. Given the nature of the Christian religion joining faith to concrete circumstances, and given the desperateness of human need in nuclear days, we cannot help assigning more of our resources to social change. There is no authentic worship of God without service to man. There is no reason for preserving the structure of the church unless it is performing its function. The policy of the church should be primarily designed not for maintenance but for mission. Yet on all these matters it has been suggested that the church is moving with all the drama of a snail taking a nap. Little more can be expected on the social front so long as the church retains its present priorities.

In the literature that the church publishes, the budgets it adopts, and the programs it plans, community witness must now play a larger part. The local church committee dealing with community concerns should be at least as active as the committee supervising the education of various ages within the church. Probably the former program should be even more extensive since there are more people and problems outside the church than inside. The ministry of laymen who are active in the community should be recognized as often as we honor church school teachers. Perhaps such "ministers on weekdays" through their sponsoring committee should report as often to the governing body of the congregation as do the committees on membership or finance. If we were to exhibit thoroughly a well-rounded church life, a congregation might not only worship together once a week, but in various subgroupings, act together at least once a week.

Before this emphasis will get very far it will need to be represented more adequately in staff time. If the second member added to the church staff is typically a director of Christian education working for most part with the nurture of those inside the church, then the third staff member added should be a minister of outreach or mission, to organize the community witness of the church. Or perhaps better, even before the third person is added the second should give half of his time to this emphasis. In a church with only one minister, a corresponding one third or one quarter of his time would be reserved for such "outside the church" activity. We do not seriously mean to join God in the world until we make such a commitment of staff, budget, and program.

A fourth legitimate expectation is that the church should point to paths of personal power through fellowship and worship. Within the Christian community we can find an environment of common purpose. We do not need to go it alone. Each of us can gain counsel, sympathy, and assistance from the fellowship of the faithful.

This does not mean that we should consider that congregation superior which always remains calm, placid, and harmonious. Any group that deals creatively with crucial matters can expect disagreement and even controversy. The more basic and important the proposed change the more widespread is the disagreement likely to be. Yet we know that when dealing with unresolved problems, out of the dynamic tension of contradictory positions comes refinement of a better solution than any participant had previously perceived. The mature layman hopes that his minister will fairly frequently disagree with him rather than always confirm his existing opinions, which he knows before God must be decidedly imperfect. One reason we safeguard freedom of the pulpit is that preaching may remain stimulating and helpful. This is the kind of climate in which growth best takes place.

At the same time fellowship can be maintained because there is fundamental agreement on matters more profound than the surface turbulence. The church among all other organizations should be best fitted for vigorous discussion of controversial issues because there is a "tie that binds" its members that is more basic than any current social or political debate. When we have shared religiously motivated experiences of study and work, when we have joined in humble prayer for God's guidance, then we are not easily divided by disagreement. Because "we are members one of another," we can each "speak the truth with his neighbor" (Eph. 4:25). If we stand together in openness before God, then it is in our conversation as Christians in the congregation that we find the words to speak to the world.

In the Christian fellowship we can also gain sustenance during trying experiences. Against established habit and entrenched interest, advocating creative change is repeatedly painful. Such pain calls for pastoral care, both for those working for change and those submitting to it. The ministry of the church is quite properly one of comfort as well as of challenge. As a matter of fact, the deepest reinforcing resources grow out of difficult experiences together. The congregation emerges in one very significant sense out of confrontation with the world. The church gains a sense of identity and unity in a common facing of opposition and resistance. We are less loyal to each other until we have been wounded by a common enemy.

In modern culture the name of the game is success, or "getting ahead" in income and status. In these terms Jesus was a colossal failure at an early age, and by turning to Jerusalem he denied himself a second chance. In some situations the Christian today is also aiming at becoming a successful failure. His goal is not amiable elegance or glamorous nonchalance in a penthouse. At the same time that the Christian stands within the world, he is also to be salt and light to the world. If a man is to make a major contribution to the world, he must go beyond the world. The Christian faith not only celebrates the values in the secular life, but it also condemns all existing shortcomings of secularism. In this kind of creative tension the servant church becomes always to a certain extent a suffering servant. Likewise in a godless world any man who responds to God must, in Bonhoeffer's phrase, "participate in the sufferings of God." The wider meaning of the fifty-third chapter of Isaiah and of the passion of Jesus suggests this to be the supreme revelation of God and the highest destiny of man. It is by faithfulness through painful experiences that life is released and culture reconstructed. Within the congregation churchmen discover that "we are afflicted in every way, but not crushed; perplexed, but not driven to despair" (II Cor. 4:8).

Supplementing the resources of human fellowship, the church provides also experiences in transforming worship. Ministry in the world is not solely a human enterprise. Churchmen do not have to make do with the existing powers of men. As we turn devotionally toward God we may enter an unexpectedly new dimension of existence, more fulfilling than the psychedelic promises of LSD because one moves in reality instead of illusion.

Modern man with all his skeptical scientism can still find meaning in personal devotions provided he recognizes a more transcendent dimension to life than man, nature, and their relationships. Even on a minimal basis, if he simply sees the necessity of making decisions in the light of the whole of reality, the ground of existence, the norm of love, or the potentialities of the future, he knows that adequate living requires reflection on these more ultimate matters. He may or he may not use traditional forms. He may reject the view of God made in the image of man, while he prefers to use a different set of inadequate words to describe what man cannot adequately comprehend. Some will still find a high form of prayer in classical contemplation. Perhaps modern man will increasingly find the higher rungs of prayer in the practice of the presence of God, a possibility seen by Brother Lawrence while he was a lay cook in a Carmelite monastery. The practice of the presence is a form of devotions that in the regular round of daily occupations continuously cultivates the capacity to relate worldly activities to more ultimate things.

A person's full resources for decision and action are not released until he stands in such openness before God in worship. There is a kind of unitary life in which personal powers are heightened because they move in a single direction instead of pulling in all directions at once. This is the well-ordered life with its vitalities in full accord because they are integrated around a central loyalty. When a man's basic theological belief, social opinion, action, and worship form a coherent whole, he not only lives a more authentic existence, but he makes more of an impact on his society. The mystics have spoken of two wings by which men rise, personal devotion and social action. We might here, too, observe, "What therefore God has joined together, let not man put asunder."

This opens a whole new range of human possibilities. Just as our physical bodies have capabilities we do not know to exist until emergencies arise, so our total personalities hold potentialities not yet released. It has been suggested that man is the missing link between the animal and the authentic human being. Even the most intelligent dogs do not build skyscrapers, and ordinary men do not find full fellowship with God. But impressive scientific research as well as spiritual experience make it increasingly clear that a higher level of humanity is possible. In religious terms a continuation of creation can reveal a new being.

The victims of a disordered world long for those who join spiritual power to social principle. "Creation waits with eager longing for the revealing of the sons of God." (Rom. 8:19.) As the child stands at the gate at the end of the day waiting for the father to appear, as airmen adrift on the sea wait for rescue when their supplies have been exhausted—so do despairing peasants in Asia, frustrated mothers in the slums, and all the disinherited of the earth yearn for the release of effective strength in the service of high purpose.

God is eager to transform the world through us. He longs to perfect a divine transmutation within us. He is more anxious to give his power than we are to receive. His grace is abundant, overflowing. If we remove the obstructions that block the channels through our lives, we can prepare for miraculously unexpected consequences.

Realizing such a potentiality requires a decisive rejection of suburban blindness and apathy. Confronted by change, threat, complexity, and resistance, many a man pulls in his antennae, protectively shuts his windows, and turns to his own private pleasures. Many of us have raised around ourselves solid walls of privilege, trying to shut out the resentful cries of exploited men. Within these isolated walls, we have fallen into a life of boredom, alienation, meaninglessness, and despair. This is the normal consequence of preoccupation with lower ranges of values predominately for one's own interests. In the same threatening situation others keep all their senses alive in outgoing concern and vigorous protest against even overwhelming odds. They find vital meaning in existence and as an unsought by-product experience the actualization of an ever wider range of their full potentialities. Instead of fake, cosmetic-thin thrills daubed on the surface of life, theirs is a depth of tranquility and happiness that is not even imagined by the hedonist. Fully alert and intensely receptive, they revel not only in the best sensations of sight and sound, but also in enlarged capacities for human sympathy and for relationship to God. This is the way human life is intended. This is what happens when one is turned on and turns out.

This is not so much a book to be read as a manual to be lived. Each churchman has before him a checklist for choice. What form of community ministry should I now more seriously enter? In addition to what I do in family and church, is there an insistent calling for me on the job, in community organizations, and in political action? No one of us can have it both ways. Either we give up the careless living and thoughtless mediocrity common among our contemporaries, or we reject the summons of God to a novel style of life with unsuspected potentialities.

The creative man realizes that anything as vast as universal peace or equal rights for all mankind begins in small places close to his home. The initial contributions are made in actions so unpromising that no one thinks them worth noting in a diary, in neighborhoods so small they cannot be seen on any map of the world. Yet, unless we begin there, we contribute to nothing of any great consequence. A creative man knows that in the existing power struggle he cannot dictate what will happen, but that he can influence the outcome of events. In ways indicated in previous chapters one man realistically joined to a group and responsive to God can put his strength behind those constructive initiatives that give significance to life.

Therefore a person can move with serenity amid the noise and the haste. He can focus on one thing amidst complexity and turbulence. With all of its hypocrisy, drudgery, and disappointment, this is still a fascinating world where one can be productive in spite of limitations and grow even because of opposition. The process of shattering indifference and intensifying involvement is a design for adventure and excitement in life. Especially in this rapid revolutionary age, one can gain a sense of participation that will to some extent alter the destinies of mankind for generations. Under such circumstances moral insensitivity is what the Bible calls hardness of heart. Creative expression in society is what our religious heritage knows to be service of God.